ECONOMIC ISSUES, PROBLEMS AND PERSPECTIVES

FEDERAL BUDGET OUTLOOK AND ECONOMIC IMPLICATIONS

Economic Issues, Problems and Perspectives

Additional books in this series can be found on Nova's website under the Series tab.

Additional E-books in this series can be found on Nova's website under the E-books tab.

American Political, Economic, and Security Issues

Additional books in this series can be found on Nova's website under the Series tab.

Additional E-books in this series can be found on Nova's website under the E-books tab.

ECONOMIC ISSUES, PROBLEMS AND PERSPECTIVES

FERDERAL BUDGET OUTLOOK AND ECONOMIC IMPLICATIONS

MICHAEL S. OKADA
EDITOR

Nova Science Publishers, Inc.
New York

For permission to use material from this book please contact us:
Telephone 631-231-7269; Fax 631-231-8175
Web Site: http://www.novapublishers.com

LIBRARY OF CONGRESSCATALOGING-IN-PUBLICATION DATA

Federal budget outlook and economic implications / editor, Michael S. Okada.
p. cm.
Includes index.
ISBN 978-1-61761-769-0 (hbk.)
1. Budget--United States.2. Government spending policy--United States.3. United States--Appropriations and expenditures. 4. United States--Economic conditions--2009- 5. United States--Economic policy--2009- I. Okada, Michael S.
HJ2051.F393 2010
336.73--dc22
2010043951

Published by Nova Science Publishers, Inc. † New York

CONTENTS

PREFACE

The federal budget is central to Congress's ability to assert its "power of the purse." Federal budget decisions express Congress's priorities among competing aims and reinforce Congress's influence on federal policies. The budget also affects, and is affected by, the national economy as a whole. The federal budget over the next few fiscal years will likely face significant challenges to both revenues and outlays as a result of recent turmoil in the economy and financial markets. This new book explores the federal budget outlook and economic implications as concerns remain about the federal government's long-term fiscal situation. The rising costs of federal health care programs and the effects of the baby boom generation's retirement present serious challenges to fiscal stability

Chapter 1- The federal budget is central to Congress's ability to assert its "power of the purse." Federal budget decisions express Congress's priorities among competing aims and reinforce Congress's influence on federal policies. The budget also affects, and is affected by, the national economy as a whole. The federal budget over the next few fiscal years will likely face significant challenges to both revenues and outlays as a result of recent turmoil in the economy and financial markets. This new book explores the federal budget outlook and economic implications as concerns remain about the federal government's long-term fiscal situation. The rising costs of federal health care programs and the effects of the baby boom generation's retirement present serious challenges to fiscal stability

Chapter 2- Following the financial crisis, the budget deficit reached 10% of GDP in 2009, a level that cannot be sustained in the long run. Concerns about long-term fiscal sustainability depend on the projected future path of the budget, absent future policy changes. The retirement of the baby boomers, rising life expectancy, and the rising cost of medical care result in projections of large and growing budget deficits over the next several decades. Social Security outlays are projected to rise from 4.8% of gross domestic product (GDP) today to 6.0% of GDP in 2035, and Medicare and Medicaid outlays are projected to rise from 5.3% today to as much as 10.0% of GDP in 2035 and 12.7% of GDP in 2050. These increases in spending are not expected to subside after the baby boomers have passed away. Without any corresponding rise in revenues, this spending path would lead to unsustainably large and persistent budget deficits, which would push up interest rates and the trade deficit, crowd out private investment spending, and ultimately cause fiscal crisis

Chapter 3- Since 1992, GAO has published long-term fiscal simulations of what might happen to federal deficits and debt levels under varying policy assumptions. We developed our long-term model in response to a bipartisan request from Members of Congress who were concerned about the long-term effects of fiscal policy. More recently, GAO has also begun publishing separate long-term fiscal simulations for the state and local government sector.

Chapter 4- In March 2010, the Congressional Budget Office (CBO) released its most recent baseline projections of federal revenues, outlays, and budget balances for the next 10 years.[1] For those projections, CBO assumed the continuation of current laws and policies that affect taxes and mandatory spending programs and extrapolated the growth of discretionary spending by using projected rates of inflation. CBO estimated in March that the baseline budget deficit will total $463billion in 2014, compared with a deficit of $1.4 trillion in 2009. The deficit was 9.9 percent of gross domestic product (GDP) in 2009—the largest share in more than half a century. By the end of 2014, CBO projects, the deficit will amount to 2.6percent of GDP if current laws and policies remain in place.

Chapter 5- The budget resolution sets forth aggregate levels of spending, revenue, and public debt. It is not intended to establish details of spending or revenue policy and does not provide levels of spending for specific agencies or programs. Instead, its purpose is to create enforceable parameters within which Congress can consider legislation dealing with spending and revenue.

The spending policies in the budget resolution encompass two types of spending legislation: discretionary spending and direct (mandatory) spending. Discretionary spending is controlled through the appropriations process. Appropriations legislation is considered each fiscal year and provides funding for numerous programs such as national defense, education, and homeland security.

Direct spending, alternately, is provided for in legislation outside of appropriations acts. Direct spending programs are typically established in permanent law and continue in effect until such time as revised or terminated by another law.

In: Federal Budget Outlook and Economic... ISBN: 978-1-61761-769-0
Editors: Michael S. Okada

Chapter 1

THE FEDERAL BUDGET: CURRENT AND UPCOMING ISSUES

D. Andrew Austin and Mindy R. Levit

SUMMARY

The federal budget helps implement Congress's "power of the purse" by expressing Congress's spending priorities among competing aims. The Obama Administration's FY2010 budget described several important changes, including increased funding for certain domestic priorities, major programmatic reforms, and proposed spending cuts in some programs. The current economic climate continues to pose major challenges to policymakers. Federal spending tied to means-tested social programs rose due to rising unemployment, while federal revenues are projected to fall as individuals' incomes have dropped and corporate profits have sunk. Federal deficits, according to OMB and CBO projections, will likely be high relative to historic norms over the next few years, as spending rises and revenues fall relative to previously anticipated levels. FY2009 outlays rose to $3,522 billion (24.9% of GDP) and revenues fell to $2,105 billion (14.7% of GDP), yielding a total federal deficit of $1,417 billion (10.0% of GDP).

Over the past decade, federal spending has accounted for approximately a fifth of the economy (as measured by gross domestic product—GDP) and federal revenues have ranged between just under a sixth to just over a fifth of

GDP. In FY2008, the U.S. government collected $2.5 trillion in revenue and spent almost $3.0 trillion. Outlays as a proportion of GDP rose from 18.4% in FY2000 to 21.0% of GDP in FY2008. Federal revenues as a proportion of GDP reached a post-WWII peak of 20.9% in FY2000 and then fell to 16.3% of GDP in FY2004 before rising slightly to 17.7% of GDP in FY2008.

The Obama Administration released the FY2010 budget outline on February 26, 2009, followed by the remaining budget documents on May 7 and 11, 2009. Major policy initiatives included new spending targeted toward health care reform, clean energy, and education. The budget resolution (S.Con.Res. 13), which followed most of the President's initiatives, was agreed to on April 29, 2009. It specified $2,322 billion in revenues and $3,555 billion in outlays, resulting in a projected FY2010 deficit of $1,233 billion. A FY2009 war funding supplemental (P.L. 111-32) was enacted in June 2009. The House passed all 12 regular FY2010 appropriations acts by the end of July 2009. The Legislative Branch appropriations bill (P.L. 111-68) enacted October 1 contained a continuing resolution to extend funding to the end of the month. On October 30, the Interior-Environment bill (P.L. 111-88), which included a second continuing resolution to extend funding until December 18, was enacted. Five remaining bills (Commerce-Justice-Science; Financial Services; Labor-HHS; Military Construction-VA; and State-Foreign Operations) were folded into the Transportation-HUD bill, creating an omnibus spending measure (H.R. 3288; P.L. 111-117) that was enacted on December 16. Finally, the defense bill (H.R. 3326; P.L. 111-118), was signed into law on December 19, finishing the regular appropriations process for FY2010.

The federal government made significant financial interventions aimed at alleviating economic recession. The final costs of federal responses to this turmoil will depend on the pace of economic recovery, how well firms with federal credit guarantees weather future financial shocks, and how much the government loses or gains on its asset purchases. Federal loans or loan guarantee programs may help provide liquidity to distressed financial markets and stimulate economic activity, but may also expose the federal government to substantial credit risks. While many economists concurred on the need for short-term fiscal stimulus despite adverse impact on the deficit, concerns remain about the federal government's long-term fiscal situation. Rising costs of federal health care programs and Baby Boomer retirements present serious challenges to fiscal stability. Operating these programs in their current form may pass on substantial economic burdens to future generations.

The federal budget is central to Congress's ability to assert its "power of the purse." Federal budget decisions express Congress's priorities among competing aims and reinforce TCongress's influence on federal policies. The budget also affects, and is affected by, the national economy as a whole. The federal budget over the next few fiscal years will likely face significant challenges to both revenues and outlays as a result of recent turmoil in the economy and financial markets.

Making budgetary decisions for the federal government is an enormously complex process, entailing the efforts of tens of thousands of staff persons in the executive and legislative branches, totaling millions of work hours each year. The budget process allows the President and Congress to negotiate and refine spending plans for the nation's fiscal priorities.[1]

The current budget situation is challenging. The federal government faces very large budget deficits, rising costs of entitlement programs, and significant spending on overseas military operations. The enactment of financial intervention and fiscal stimulus legislation designed to alleviate a credit crunch and to bolster the economy will push up the deficit, shifting fiscal burdens into the future. While GDP grew at an estimated annual rate of 2.8% in the third quarter of 2009, perhaps marking an end to the longest post-World War II recession, most forecasters expect unemployment to remain at high levels for the medium term.[2] The Congressional Budget Office (CBO) projects that the unemployment rate will crest at nearly 10.5% in early 2010, well above some earlier predictions.[3] High unemployment rates would add to government spending through "automatic stabilizer" programs, such as unemployment insurance and income support programs.

The economic downturn has not only pushed federal spending up and revenues down, but also threatens to slow economic growth for the next few years. The federal government has responded to the economic slowdown with an array of policy responses unprecedented in recent decades, including fiscal stimulus and loan programs. These federal interventions have helped stimulate economic activity and reduce dislocation in financial markets, but may also expose the federal government to substantial credit risks.

Concern remains about the federal government's long-term fiscal situation. The rising costs of federal health care programs and the effects of the baby boom generation's retirement present serious challenges to fiscal stability. Operating these programs in their current form may pass on substantial economic burdens to future generations.

OVERVIEW

Revenues, Outlays, and Deficits for FY2008

Over the past decade, federal spending has accounted for approximately a fifth of the economy (as measured by gross domestic product—GDP) and federal revenues have ranged between just under a sixth and just over a fifth of GDP, as shown in **Figure 1**. In FY2008, the U.S. government collected $2.5 trillion in revenue and spent almost $3.0 trillion. Outlays as a proportion of GDP rose from 18.4% in FY2000 to 21.0% of GDP in FY2008.[4] Federal revenues as a proportion of GDP reached a post-WWII peak of 20.9% in FY2000 and then fell to 16.3% of GDP in FY2004 before rising to 17.7% of GDP in FY2008.

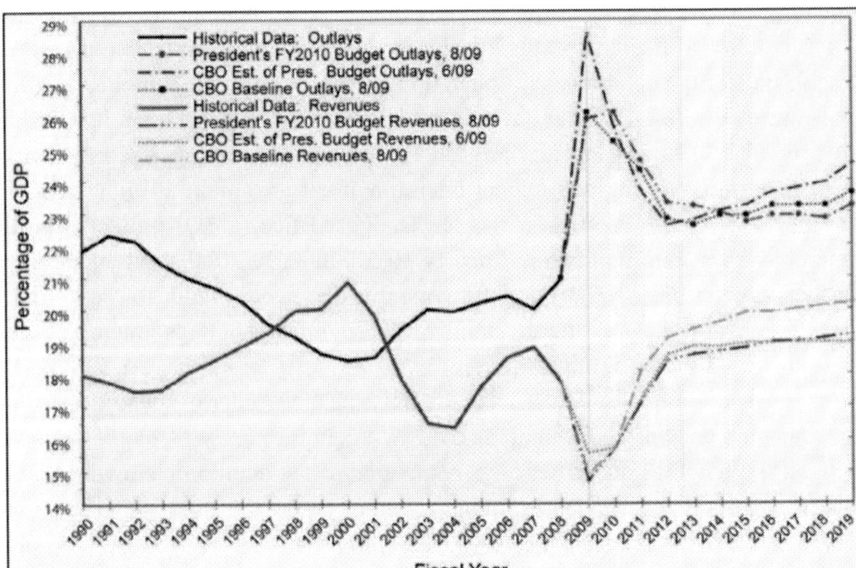

Source: CBO, *Historical Tables*, available at http://www.cbo.gov/budget/historical.shtml; *An Analysis of the President's Budgetary Proposals for Fiscal Year 2010*, June 2009, available at http://www.cbo.gov/doc.cfm?index= 10296; *The Budget and Economic Outlook: An Update*, August 2009, available at http://www.cbo.gov/doc.cfm?index= 10521; OMB, *Budget for Fiscal Year 2010 Mid-Session Review*, Table S-1, August 2009, available at http://www.whitehouse.gov/omb/budget/MSR/. Data for FY2009 are estimates and data for FY2010-FY2019 are projections.

Figure 1. Total Outlays and Revenues as a Percentage of GDP, FY1990-FY2019

The annual budget deficit (or surplus) is revenue (i.e., taxes and fees) that the government collects minus outlays (i.e., spending).[5] The total deficit in FY2008 was $459 billion, or 3.2% of gross domestic product (GDP), sharply higher than the FY2007 deficit of $162 billion. The U.S. Treasury Department, on October 16, 2009, announced that the FY2009 total deficit reached $1,417 billion, or 10.0% of GDP.[6] While large by historical standards, the FY2009 deficit was somewhat smaller than the Administration had expected in August 2009 ($1,580 billion, or 11.2% of GDP) and much smaller than the $1,752 billion deficit projected in the President's budget submission.[7] The actual FY2009 budget deficit was smaller than previous estimates in large part because the $250 billion included in the Administration's budget proposals for additional intervention in financial markets was not spent.[8]

The total deficit, according to some budget experts, gives an incomplete view of the government's fiscal condition because it includes Social Security surpluses (which are then held in Treasury trust funds until used to pay future benefits). Excluding off-budget items (Social Security benefits paid net of Social Security payroll taxes collected and the U.S. Postal Service's net balance) the (on-budget) FY2008 federal deficit was $642 billion. The August 2009 CBO estimate of the FY2009 on-budget deficit, at $1,720 billion, was even higher. The estimation of federal deficits is complicated by the difficulties in estimating the costs of major federal interventions in the latter half of 2008, such as the creation of the TARP and placing the mortgage giants Fannie Mae and Freddie Mac under conservatorship.[9]

Trends

FederalSpending

Budget enforcement legislation divides federal outlays into discretionary and mandatory spending, as well as net interest.[10] Discretionary spending flows from and is controlled by annual congressional appropriations acts. Mandatory spending encompasses federal government spending on entitlement programs, the Supplemental Nutrition Assistance Program (SNAP; formerly the Food Stamp program), and other spending controlled by laws other than annual appropriation acts.

Outlays rose from 20.6% of GDP in FY2008 to 24.8% of GDP in FY2009. Over time, mandatory spending has generally grown faster than discretionary spending. As Figure 2 shows, mandatory spending, which equaled 11.2% of GDP in FY2008, totaled 16.1% of GDP in FY2009, or almost two-thirds of total outlays. TARP spending and costs linked to the deprivatization of mortgage giants Fannie Mae and Freddie Mac accounted for much of the increase in mandatory spending. CBO projects that FY2019 mandatory spending will total 13.1% of GDP, reflecting a sharp decrease in financial stabilization costs and long-term growth in entitlement spending. Discretionary spending as a share of GDP fell in the 1990s, but rose from 6.3% of GDP in FY2000 to 8.0% of GDP in FY2008 and 8.8% of GDP in FY2009. By 2019, according to CBO baseline projections (which assume that discretionary spending remains constant in real terms), discretionary spending will fall to 7.0% of GDP.[11]

Discretionary outlays increased 4.3% a year on average in real terms from FY1999 to FY2008. The share of discretionary spending as a proportion of total federal outlays rose from 33.6% in FY1999 to 38.0% in FY2008. Higher defense outlays accounted for 64.6% of the increase in discretionary spending over the past decade. On average, from FY1999 to FY2008, defense outlays grew 5.5% per year in real terms, while real non-defense discretionary outlays grew 3.1% per year.

Entitlement programs such as Social Security and Medicare make up the bulk of mandatory spending.[12] Other mandatory spending programs include Temporary Assistance to Needy Families (TANF), Supplemental Security Income (SSI), unemployment insurance, veterans' benefits, federal employee retirement and disability, SNAP (formerly Food Stamps), and the Earned Income Tax Credit (EITC). Congress sets eligibility requirements and benefits for entitlement programs, rather than appropriating a fixed sum each year. Therefore, if the eligibility requirements are met for a specific mandatory program, outlays are made automatically.

Over the past 40 years, mandatory spending has taken up a larger and larger share of the federal budget. In 1962, before the 1965 creation of Medicare and Medicaid, less than 30% of all federal spending was mandatory. At that time, Social Security accounted for about half of all mandatory spending. By FY2008, mandatory spending had grown to 53.7% of total outlays, with Social Security, Medicare, and the federal share of Medicaid alone comprising over 43% of all federal spending. Discretionary spending totaled 38.0% in FY2008. Net interest payments accounted for the remaining 8.3% of total spending.

Because discretionary spending is now at a historic low as a proportion of total federal outlays, some budget experts contend that any significant reductions in federal spending must include mandatory spending cuts. Other budget and social policy experts contend that cuts in mandatory spending would cause substantial disruption to many households because mandatory spending funds important parts of the social safety net.

Federal Revenue

Individual income taxes have long been the largest source of federal revenues, followed by social insurance taxes. Federal individual and corporate income tax revenues typically track broader trends in the economy. In FY2008, individual income tax revenues totaled $1,146 billion (8.1% of GDP), comprising about 45% of total federal revenues. In FY2009, difficult economic conditions led individual income tax revenue to fall to $918 billion (6.5% of GDP). Corporate income tax revenues fell from $304 billion in FY2008 to $138 billion in FY2009. Federal revenues from other sources fell as well, although much less dramatically.[13]

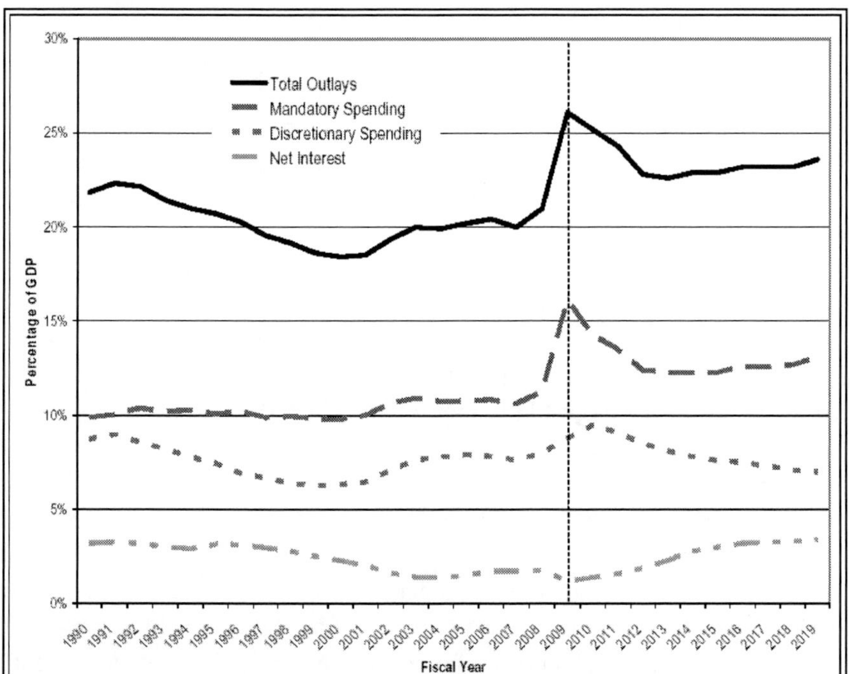

Source: CBO, *Historical Tables*, available at http://www.cbo.gov/ budget/ historical.shtml and *The Budget and Economic Outlook: An Update*, August 2009, available at http://www.cbo.gov/doc.cfm?index=10521. Data for FY2009 are estimates and data for FY2010-FY2019 are projections.

Figure 2. Outlays by Type as a Percentage of GDP, FY1990-FY2019

Deficits, Debt, and Interest

The federal government's fiscal stance is often gauged by the annual budget deficit. The budget deficit, however, may give a partial and potentially misleading picture of the government's fiscal condition.[14] Annual budget deficits or surpluses determine, over time, the level of federal debt and affect the growth of interest payments to finance the debt.

FederalDeficits

Deficits can serve as a powerful instrument of fiscal policy. Differences between revenues and outlays determine whether or not the budget is in surplus or deficit, which often serves as a measure of the federal government's fiscal health. Annual budget deficits or surpluses determine, over time, the level of federal debt and affect the amount of annual interest paid to finance the debt. Occasional deficits, in and of themselves, are not necessarily problematic. Deficit spending allows governments to smooth outlays and taxes to shield taxpayers and program beneficiaries from abrupt economic shocks in the short term. Persistent deficits, however, lead to growing accumulations of federal debt that may lead to higher interest payments, tax increases, or spending cuts, and may also have adverse macroeconomic consequences in the long term.[15]

Deficit projections for the next several fiscal years are high relative to historic standards. The deficit reached its peak in FY1943 at 30.3% of GDP. After WWII, deficits remained relatively low until the mid-1980s. In FY1985, the deficit reached 6.0% of GDP. The FY2009 total deficit was $1,417 billion (10.0% of GDP), the largest in proportion to GDP since FY1946.[16]

FederalDebt

Gross federal debt is composed of debt held by the public and intragovernmental debt.[17]Intragovernmental debt is the amount owed by the Federal government to other federal agencies, to be paid by the Department of the Treasury. This amount largely consists of money contained in trust funds, such as Social Security, that has been invested in Federal securities as required by law.[18] Debt held by the public is the total amount the Federal government has borrowed from the public and remains outstanding. This measure is generally considered to be the most relevant in macroeconomic terms because it is the amount of debt sold in credit markets.

Changes in debt held by the public generally track the movements of the annual on-budget deficits and surpluses. Whether or not the movements of gross federal debt will follow those of debt held by the public depends on how intergovernmental debt changes. Higher debt levels could slow investment and lower economic growth.[19]

DebtLimit

Congress sets a ceiling on federal debt through a legislatively established limit that helps Congress assert its constitutional prerogative to control spending. The debt limit also imposes a form of fiscal accountability that compels Congress and the President to take visible action, in the form of a vote authorizing a debt limit increase, to allow further federal borrowing when nearing the statutory limit. The debt limit can hinder the Treasury's ability to manage the federal government's finances when the amount of federal debt approaches this ceiling. In those instances, the Treasury has had to take unusual and extraordinary measures to meet federal obligations.[20] While the debt limit has never caused the federal government to default on its obligations, it has caused inconvenience and uncertainty in Treasury operations at times.

On February 17, 2009, the American Recovery and Reinvestment Act of 2009 (H.R. 1, P.L. 111-5) increased the debt limit to $12,104 billion. As of October 26, 2009, federal debt subject to limit was approximately $11,898 billion, of which, $7,475 billion was held by the public. CBO had estimated that federal debt subject to limit would reach the limit then in place ($12,104 billion) in the last months of calendar year 2009. In August 2009, according to media reports, Treasury Secretary Geithner wrote Congress to warn that the federal debt would soon reach its legal limit and urged Congress to raise the debt limit.[21] The Treasury, however, announced in November that the debt limit would probably not be reached until mid to late December.[22] Rather than passing the debt limit measure (H.J.Res. 45) automatically generated in the House by passage of the budget resolution, Congress chose to increase the limit by a smaller amount sufficient to let the U.S. Treasury pursue normal debt management policies for two months or so. H.R. 4314, passed by the House on December 16, 2009, and by the Senate on December 24, raised the debt limit to $12.394 trillion when the President signed the measure on December 28.[23]

Net Interest

In FY2008, the U.S. spent $253 billion, or 1.8% of GDP, on net interest payments on the debt. What the government pays in interest depends on market interest rates as well as on the size and composition of the federal debt.

Since FY1968, the U.S. spent an average of 2.2% of GDP on interest payments. In FY2004, interest payments dipped to a low of 1.4% of GDP. If the value of the federal debt in real terms were to grow faster than the economy, the burden of paying interest on the debt would grow as well.

Currently, low interest rates have held down net interest payments as a percentage of GDP relative to the historical average. CBO projects net interest payments for FY2009 will fall to 1.2% of GDP, despite increases in borrowing to finance the deficit.[24] Some economists, however, have expressed concern that federal interest costs could rise sharply once the economy recovers, resulting in future strain on the budget.[25]

Budget Cycle

A single year's budget cycle takes roughly three calendar years from initial formation by the Office of Management and Budget (OMB) until final audit.[26] The executive agencies begin the budget process by compiling detailed budget requests in the calendar year before the President's budget submission. Many agencies start working on their budgets during the spring and summer—about year and a half before the fiscal year begins. OMB oversees the development of these agency requests. The President, by law, must submit a budget, which is based on OMB's work, by the first Monday in February.[27]

Because this date followed Inauguration Day so closely, the Obama Administration had little time to compile budget documents. In past decades, some new presidents relied on their predecessors' budget teams to outline a budgetary framework for submission in February and then submit their own budget or revisions at a later date.[28] The Obama Administration presented an outline of the FY2010 budget on February 26, 2009, and submitted its full budget proposal on May 7 and 11, 2009.

Congress typically begins formal consideration of the budget once the President submits his budget request. This year House and Senate Budget Committees began work on budget resolutions in March, even though the President's full budget submission had not yet been submitted. The budget resolution sets out a plan, agreed to by the House and Senate, that establishes the framework for subsequent budget legislation.

House and Senate Appropriations Committees and their subcommittees typically begin work on bills that fund discretionary spending programs once the budget resolution is agreed upon. Appropriations Committees review agency funding requests and propose levels of budget authority (BA).

Appropriations acts passed by Congress set the amount of BA available for specific programs and activities. Authorizing committees, which control mandatory spending, and committees with jurisdiction over revenues also play important roles in budget decision-making.

During the fiscal year, which begins on October 1, Congress and OMB oversee the execution of the budget. Once the fiscal year ends on the following September 30, the Treasury Department and the Government Accountability Office (GAO) begin year-end audits.

Budget Baseline Projections

The Congressional Budget Office (CBO) provides data and analysis to Congress throughout the budget and appropriations process. Each January, CBO issues a *Budget and Economic Outlook* that contains current-law baseline estimates of outlays and revenues. In March, CBO typically issues an analysis of the President's budget submission with revised baseline estimates and projections. OMB issues a *Mid-Session Review* in July with budget data revised to reflect changes in policy proposals, changed economic conditions, and other factors. In late summer, CBO issues an updated *Budget and Economic Outlook* with new baseline projections.

Due to changing economic conditions and the enactment of major legislation in the early part of 2009, CBO also posted interim analyses as requested by Congress in order to provide more up-to-date projections of the fiscal outlook between the release of its January and March baselines.[29] These legislative changes as well as revised economic assumptions were incorporated into CBO's March 2009 *A Preliminary Analysis of the President's Budget and an Update of CBO's Budget and Economic Outlook.*[30] CBO revised its estimates of the President's policies in June 2009 in its report, *An Analysis of the President's Budgetary Proposals for Fiscal Year 2010.*[31] CBO released a revised budget and economic outlook on August 25.[32]

The CBO current-law baseline sets a benchmark to evaluate whether legislative proposals would increase or decrease outlays and revenue collection. Baseline estimates are not intended to predict likely future outcomes, but to show what spending and revenues would be if current law remained in effect. CBO typically evaluates the budgetary consequences of legislative proposals and the Joint Committee on Taxation (JCT) evaluates the consequences of revenue proposals.

CBO computes baseline projections using certain assumptions.[33] Forecasts based on these assumptions typically yield higher revenue estimates and slower growth of discretionary spending relative to scenarios independent forecasters consider likely. More specifically, CBO baseline projections incorporate three legislatively mandated assumptions: that discretionary spending remains constant in inflation-adjusted terms, that the 2001 and 2003 tax cuts fully expire after 2010 (as current law specifies), and that one-year "patches" to the alternative minimum tax (AMT) will lapse even though past Congresses have extended AMT patches year after year. However, CBO does provide projections of these costs separately from its baseline. In addition to these legislative assumptions, macroeconomic assumptions, namely the point at which CBO expects the recession to end, will also affect the baseline estimates and projections especially given the current economic climate.

Previous baseline projections showed substantial growth in receipts after 2010, when most of the tax cuts from 2001 and 2003 expire. Federal deficits are expected to grow rapidly beyond the 10-year forecast window unless major policy changes are made, however, largely because of increased outlays due to rapidly growing health care costs and Baby Boomer retirements.

Budgeting in Tough Economic Times: The FY2009 and FY2010 Budgets

Aside from the specific issues related to the budget in presidential transition years, the current economic climate poses another major challenge to policymakers shaping the federal budget. Federal spending tied to means-tested social programs has been increasing due to rising unemployment, while federal revenues will likely fall as individuals' incomes drop and corporate profits sink.

Financial and Economic Turmoil

Financial markets have been in turmoil since August 2007. That turmoil intensified in March 2008 when the investment bank Bear Stearns was forced to sell itself to JPMorgan Chase, and intensified again on September 7, when government-sponsored mortgage guarantors Fannie Mae and Freddie Mac were placed into conservatorship. A week later, on September 15, 2008, the investment bank Lehman Brothers declared bankruptcy. The next day, the Federal Reserve extended an $85 billion loan to the insurance giant AIG to avoid its collapse. AIG subsequently received additional capital injections by the Federal Reserve.[34] In the week following the Lehman bankruptcy and AIG's near-death experience, equity markets experienced sharp declines and money markets and commercial paper markets experienced severe disruptions.[35]

Financial turmoil and declining residential real estate markets in late 2007 soon led to broader economic problems. The U.S. economy, according to the National Bureau of Economic Research (NBER), entered a recession in December 2007, which has been longer and deeper than any other since the Great Depression. Real GDP grew an estimated annual rate of 2.8% in the third quarter of 2009, marking an end to the longest post-World War II recession. The November 2009 Blue Chip consensus forecasts projected that real GDP will grow at a 2.7% annual pace and the unemployment rate will average nearly 10% in calendar year 2010.[36] Most forecasters expect unemployment, which is generally considered a lagging indicator of economic activity, to remain at high levels for the medium term. CBO projects that the unemployment rate will peak in early 2010 just shy of 10.5%.[37]

Federal Response to Turmoil in 2008 and 2009

The federal government has responded to this financial turmoil with an extraordinary set of measures. In February 2008, Congress enacted a $152 billion package (P.L. 110-185, Economic Stimulus Act of 2008) to stimulate consumption that sent refunds to taxpayers and let firms depreciate their capital more quickly. Later in the year, the Federal Reserve created a panoply of lending facilities, such as the Term Auction Facility (TAF), the Primary Dealer Credit Facility (PDCF), and the Term Securities Lending Facility (TSLF), among others. These facilities provide financial institutions with loans in exchange for various types of collateral.

On October 3, Congress passed the Emergency Economic Stabilization Act of 2008 (EESA; P.L. 110-343), which authorized the Treasury Secretary to use $700 billion (subject to certain congressional restrictions and notifications) to intervene in financial markets or to inject capital into key financial institutions as part of a Troubled Assets Relief Program (TARP). While Treasury Secretary Henry Paulson first proposed using TARP funds to buy mortgage-related securities, those plans were later shelved. Instead, the

Treasury Department injected TARP funds to recapitalize banks and financial institutions by acquiring preferred shares. On November 12, Paulson announced that a portion of TARP would fund a new Federal Reserve collateralized lending program, the Term Asset-Backed Securities Loan Facility (TALF), which will take in securities based on "newly and recently originated" loans, such as for education, automobiles, and credit cards. Treasury Secretary Geithner announced details of a plan to use TARP funds, in cooperation with the Public-Private Investment Program (PPIP), to purchase legacy (i.e., troubled) assets in March 2009.[38] By early November 2009, six investment firms had qualified for PPIP and another three firms were reportedly close to qualifying.[39]

Additional efforts to jump-start economic growth came in the form of another stimulus package passed by Congress on February 13, 2009, and signed into law by President Obama on February 17, 2009. The American Recovery and Reinvestment Act of 2009 (ARRA; H.R. 1, P.L. 111-5) includes provisions that, according to CBO, would total $787.2 billion in increased spending and reduced taxes over the FY2009-FY2019 period or just over 5% of GDP in 2008.[40] ARRA includes support for state and local governments in the form of increased infrastructure, Medicaid, school funding, funding for health care IT, extended unemployment benefits, as well as tax cuts and rebates among other provisions.[41]

The size, variety, and complexity of federal responses to financial and economic turmoil present many challenges to budget analysis. The ultimate costs of these responses will depend on how the economy performs, how well firms with federal credit guarantees weather future financial shocks, and whether or not the government receives positive returns on its asset purchases. Estimating how much these responses will cost the federal government is difficult, both for conceptual and operational reasons.

WhatCounts As an Outlay?

The distinction between outlays and budget authority is important to understanding the budgetary consequences of federal responses to economic and financial turmoil. Outlays are disbursed federal funds. Budget authority, as determined by what Congress appropriates, is what federal agencies can legally spend. Budget authority has been compared to funds deposited into a checking account, which then can be used for federal purposes. Giving federal officials the ability to spend requires budget authority. Until the federal government disburses funds to make purchases, however, no outlays occur. Outlays will not increase until those funds are actually disbursed.

Outlay data are used to assess the macroeconomic effects of the federal budgets, while budget analysis of specific federal programs is typically based on budget authority figures. Appropriations legislation is generally framed in terms of budget authority because that is what Congress can most directly control.

Estimating the precise budgetary impact of programs like TARP is difficult. For example, much of the early amounts of TARP funds were used to purchase preferred equity stakes in major banks. EESA requires those equity purchases to be costed on a net present value basis with an adjustment for market risk, so that the future sale of those equity stakes would offset much of the cost of acquiring them.[42] Under the Bush Administration, OMB argued for a cash basis approach, so that those equity purchases would increase the federal deficit for FY2009 and future sales would reduce deficits in out-years as those equity stakes are sold off. Under the Obama Administration, however, OMB Director Peter Orszag adopted the scoring practices he advocated while head of CBO, thus eliminating some of the previous divergence between CBO and OMB budget estimates. Even though the value of TARP purchases is now being estimated on a net present value basis by CBO and OMB, differences still remain, which illustrate the complexity in evaluating their true cost. OMB estimated TARP outlays on a net present value basis at $235 billion in FY2009 and $70 billion in FY2010 (with further outlays beyond FY2010).[43] CBO estimates the value of these outlays, on that basis, at $133 billion in FY2009 and $80 billion in FY2010.[44]

The final scope of many elements of the financial intervention programs remains unclear given that the Treasury Secretary has been granted wide discretion in how to use these funds. Outside of TARP, other federal agencies have also used their statutory authority to provide relief to the financial sector and credit markets in various ways. The ultimate costs and budgetary implications depend on the strength or weakness of the economic recovery and what, if any, additional federal resources are put toward dealing with the current economic and fiscal issues with or without additional congressional action.[45]

CurrentFederal Budget Scoring Ignores SomeCreditRisks

The federal government has provided credit guarantees to several firms to reduce systematic financial or economic risks to the economy. The cost of making these guarantees to the government, however, may be much less than the value of the guarantees. If economic conditions improve soon, those credit guarantees will not result in new federal outlays. On the other hand, if the economic conditions deteriorate, the government may face major losses. The Federal Credit Reform Act of 1990 (FCRA) requires that the reported budgetary cost of credit programs equal the estimated subsidy cost at the time the credit is provided.[46] FCRA subsidy calculations, however, omit risk adjustments (except for TARP funds, as noted above).[47] The true economic cost of federal credit guarantees can be substantially underestimated when risk adjustments are omitted.[48] CBO and OMB include risk adjustments in estimates of the costs associated with the TARP as mandated by EESA.[49]

Some economists argue that the federal government should not charge for the risks it accepts. That argument, however, properly applies only to diversifiable risks—that is, risks that can be minimized by pooling small risks. For non-diversifiable risks, such as systematic risks to financial markets, governments may spread or redistribute risks, but cannot eliminate them via pooling. Some argued that because the U.S. government can borrow at a risk-free rate, that budget accounting for federal credit programs should not include a risk premium.[50] The U.S. Treasury's ability to borrow funds cheaply, however, derives from the government's ability to tax. The U.S. government can borrow at a risk-free rate not because it can eliminate risks, but because it can transfer risks to taxpayers and program beneficiaries.[51]

Federal responses to financial turmoil and the recession may expose the government to significant credit risks. Large amounts of difficult-to-value financial assets have been put on the Treasury and Federal Reserve balance sheets. Estimating scale and market cost of those risks is difficult because the way some programs will be administered is unclear. Potential costs also depend on how quickly the economy recovers and how the structure of financial markets evolves.[52]

Budget Fiscal Year 2009

Recent economic issues and resulting legislation enacted to reduce the impact of the housing and credit crises have profoundly altered the budgetary landscape. Financial turmoil and the recession will also affect outlay and revenue projections over the next several years. Any additional measures, such as further financial intervention, could impact the budget and budget balance in FY2009 and beyond.

During the past several budgetary cycles, Congress did not pass all of the regular appropriations bills, which determine discretionary spending, before the start of the fiscal year. The FY2009 budget cycle was no exception. Congress provided its budgetary outline in the budget resolution adopted in early June 2008, which called for $1,183 billion in discretionary spending and

$1,883 billion in mandatory spending. Although the budget resolution is not law, it constrains spending plans and thus plays a central role in determining budgetary outcomes.[53] Regular appropriations bills for Defense, Homeland Security, and Military Construction were included in the Consolidated Security, Disaster Assistance, and Continuing Appropriations Act of 2009 (P.L. 110-329), which was signed into law on September 30, 2008, the day before the start of FY2009. The act also provided continuing appropriations for other parts of the government until March 6, 2009. To complete FY2009 funding, the House passed the Omnibus Appropriations Act of 2009 (H.R. 1105) on February 25, 2009, on a 245-178 vote. Passage in the Senate was delayed, requiring an additional stop-gap measure (H.J.Res. 38, P.L. 111-6) to provide funding until March 11, 2009. The Senate passed the omnibus bill on a voice vote on March 10, 2009, and the President signed it the next day (P.L. 111-8), which completed regular FY2009 appropriations.

FY2009 Supplemental Appropriations

War Funding[54]

Costs of the wars in Iraq and Afghanistan have been funded for the most part by emergency supplemental appropriations since 2001. By contrast, most of the funding for the Vietnam war after the first few years was provided in regular appropriations.[55] Since 2004, war funding has been requested in two parts: an emergency "bridge" fund to cover the first part of the year that has been included as emergency appropriations in the Department of Defense's (DOD's) regular appropriations and a supplemental that has been submitted later in the fiscal year. The Supplemental Appropriations Act, FY2008 (P.L. 110-252) provided both the second part of war funding for FY2008 bringing the annual total to $187 billion, and $66 billion to cover the first part of FY2009.[56]

On April 9, 2009, the Obama Administration requested $83.4 billion for a FY2009 supplemental including $75.5 billion to fund DOD's war costs in Afghanistan and Iraq, $7.1 billion for primarily war-related foreign aid, and $0.4 billion for other needs.[57] Coupled with previously appropriated war funding, the request would bring the DOD total for FY2009 to $141.4 billion. Presumably this request reflects the President's decision to send an additional 21,000 troops to Afghanistan "to stabilize a deteriorating situation" and to reduce the number of Brigade Combat Teams in Iraq by two, a decrease of about 18,000 troops in FY2009.[58] According to OMB, this should be the last war-related supplemental. Funding for war costs in FY2010 was submitted along with the regular budget on May 7, 2009.

The Administration submitted three additional requests for supplemental funds including funds for pandemic flu preparedness and response measures, to cover potential risks to the Treasury from expanding the U.S. contribution to the borrowing authority of the International Monetary Fund, and additional funds for unanticipated needs for influenza. Together with the initial April 9 proposal, this brought the total Administration request for the FY2009 supplemental to $92.145 billion. By June 18, both the Senate and the House passed the final version of the bill (Supplemental Appropriations Act 2009; H.R. 2346), totaling $105.9 billion.[59] As often happens with supplementals, the FY2009 supplemental included not only much of the additional funding requested by the Administration, but also other funding added by Congress. President Obama signed the FY2009 supplemental (P.L. 111-32) on June 24.

Supplemental war appropriations complicate the budget process. First, some argue that war funding should be included in DOD's regular appropriations. DOD and others have suggested that war costs remain fluid and that combining regular and war appropriations could make the administrative and budgetary segregation of war funding and the costs of DOD's baseline peacetime program more difficult. Some contend that the George W. Bush Administration used supplemental appropriations to obscure the costs of wars in Iraq and Afghanistan to the public. Second, the irregular timing of supplemental appropriations requests complicates comparisons of baseline budget forecasts. Supplementals have also been criticized for making it easier to add unrelated spending items that would be more difficult to pass individually, which is particularly the case for supplemental acts that provide funds to support troops engaged in war.

According to the terms of budget enforcement conventions, CBO baseline presumes that discretionary spending levels will continue, as enacted, for the following fiscal year in real (i.e., inflation-adjusted) terms. If these projections are run when Congress has only enacted bridge funding to cover part of the year, the baseline is likely to understate the full amount of spending for the Department of Defense. On the other hand, if the baseline is run after a supplemental is passed and an overall decline in U.S. military operations is anticipated because the drawdown in Iraq is expected to be greater than the increase in Afghanistan, then assuming the same level of war funding may overstate total defense spending. In either case, when the amount for defense spending includes war funding, it overstates the amount needed to carry on

DOD's ongoing baseline peacetime program, and will not capture any changes in U.S. military operations for overseas contingencies.

Finally, many in Congress have questioned whether after seven years, war appropriations are appropriately categorized as "unanticipated" emergencies not subject to caps in annual congressional budget resolutions. Although Congress required a full year's war request starting in FY2008, the Bush Administration failed to submit one for FY2009 (Sec. 1007, P.L. 110-364).

"Cash for Clunkers"

In addition to the war funding supplemental discussed above, the House passed a second supplemental appropriations measure (H.R. 3435) to extend the "Cash for Clunkers" program on July 31 on a 316-109 vote. The Senate approved the measure on August 6 on a 60-37 vote and it was signed into law by the President on August 7, 2009 (P.L. 111-47).[60] To pay for this extension, Congress transferred $2 billion of ARRA funds into "cash for clunkers." This program was successful in stimulating auto sales, however some have expressed skepticism of any fuel efficiency gains that will be generated. The program, initially planned to end November 1, 2009, only lasted until August 24, 2009, due to concerns that the program would run out of funds.

WhyDid Budget DeficitEstimates for FY2009 Change?

Both CBO and OMB revised their budget deficit estimates for FY2009 downward in their August releases of *The Budget and Economic Outlook: An Update* and the *Mid-Session Review*, respectively. In its baseline figures issued in March, CBO had estimated an FY2009 deficit of $1,667 billion. A revised CBO estimate released in August 2009 put the FY2009 federal deficit at $1,587 billion. The $80 billion reduction in the estimated federal deficit between March and August was in large part due to changes in estimated TARP subsidy costs, which fell by $203 billion. On the other hand, estimated revenues also fell by $85 billion between March and August, while legislative changes increased estimated defense outlays by $25 billion.[61]

The revisions in the OMB proposed budget deficit estimates, from a May FY2009 deficit estimate of $1,841 billion to an August estimate of $1,580 billion, are largely a result of the elimination of the $250 billion placeholder for additional financial stabilization efforts. OMB determined that the increased stability in the financial markets provided indication that the placeholder was no longer needed. In addition, OMB also reduced projected outlays for FDIC's deposit insurance program by $78 billion due to improved conditions in the banking industry. Offsetting these lower outlays is an $83 billion decline in revenues due to revised economic and technical assumptions.[62]

Budget Fiscal Year 2010

The Obama Administration released an outline of the FY2010 budget on February 26, 2009, the full budget proposal on May 7 and 11, 2009, and the Mid-Session Review on August 25, 2009. Using the President's February outline, Congress began its consideration of the FY2010 budget in late March 2009. Versions of the budget resolution were agreed to in the House (H.Con.Res. 85) and Senate (S.Con.Res. 13) on April 2, 2009. The Conference Report on the budget resolution (S.Con.Res. 13) was agreed to on April 29, 2009.

As of July 30, 2009, the House had passed all 12 regular appropriations acts. As of November 24, the Senate had passed nine regular appropriations acts, and of those, five have been signed into law. The Legislative Branch appropriations bill (P.L. 111-68), enacted October 1, 2009, contained a continuing resolution to extend funding to the end of the month. The Agriculture appropriations bill was enacted on October 21, followed by the Homeland Security and Energy-Water appropriations bills, which were both signed into law on October 28, 2009. On October 30, 2009, the Interior-Environment appropriations bill (P.L. 111-88), which included a second continuing resolution to extend funding until December 18, became the fifth regular appropriations bill to be signed into law.[63]

Five of the remaining regular appropriations bills (Commerce-Justice-Science; Financial Services; Labor-HHS; Military Construction-VA; and State-Foreign Operations) were folded into the Transportation-HUD bill, creating an omnibus spending measure (H.R. 3288). The House agreed to the conference report on the omnibus bill by a vote of 221-202 on December 10, and the Senate agreed to the measure on December 13. The President signed the bill on December 16, which became P.L. 111-117. The defense bill (H.R. 3326), the last regular appropriations bill to pass, was approved through an exchange of amendments between the House and Senate that concluded on December 19. The President signed the bill on the same day, which became P.L. 111-118, finishing the regular appropriations process for FY2010.

Obama Administration FY2010 Budget

The Administration's FY2010 budget contains five volumes: (1) *A New Era of Responsibility: Renewing America's Promise*; (2) *Historical Tables*; (3) *Analytical Perspectives*; (4) *Appendix*; and (5) *Terminations, Reductions, and Savings*.[64] These documents lay out the Administration's projections of the fiscal outlook for the country, along with spending levels proposed for each of the federal government's departments and programs. The *Historical Tables* volume also provides significant amounts of budget data, much of which extends back to 1962 or earlier.

In an attempt to present a full picture of the current and future fiscal outlook, the Obama Administration provided three separate deficit projections.[65] First, OMB projected a Budget Enforcement Act (BEA) baseline, using methods that mirror those CBO uses to project its current-law baseline. The BEA baseline presumes that discretionary spending remains constant in real (i.e., inflation-adjusted) terms, the 2001 and 2003 Bush Administration tax cuts expire in 2010, and that the alternative minimum tax (AMT) will not be "patched."[66] Many budget analysts believe such current law projections offer an overly rosy scenario of the long term budget pictured.[67] Under this scenario, the FY2010 deficit was projected to total $1,426 billion.

The Obama Administration also projected a Current Policy Baseline, which in its view, provides a more transparent and realistic reflection of the federal government's current fiscal situation. They also propose to continue using this methodology as a base for future budget enforcement purposes and as a mechanism for understanding how new policy choices effect the fiscal outlook, essentially replacing the current BEA baseline. The Administration's Current Policy Baseline presumes that the 2001 and 2003 tax cuts will be extended, that the alternative minimum tax (AMT) will be "patched," that certain Medicare physician payments will not be cut. This baseline also includes costs for overseas contingency operations and estimated average annual costs of major disasters, as well as an adjustment for the conversion of Pell Grants from discretionary to mandatory spending. The deficit under this scenario would reach $1,449 billion in FY2010.

The final deficit projection, the Proposed Budget, illustrates the impact on the budget outlook if all of the policies of the Obama Administration are implemented. In FY2010, the Administration projects that the deficit would reach $1,502 billion. Both the Current Policy Baseline and the Proposed Budget project deficits throughout the 10-year budget window, with deficits peaking in FY2009 and then remaining stable, as a percentage of GDP, in the out-years.

In his budget for FY2010, President Obama also presented a wide ranging policy agenda. The main policy initiatives he emphasized include significant spending and investment targeted toward health care reform, clean energy, and education.

Health Care Reform

In its budget documents, the Obama Administration argues that achieving health care reform is necessary to stabilize the federal government's fiscal condition for the long-run. Spending on health programs, such as Medicare and Medicaid, is projected to comprise a larger and larger proportion of the federal budget.

Congress continues to consider major reforms of the health insurance and health care system, designed to expand access to health insurance and health care, to improve the quality of health care, and to slow the growth of health care costs.[68] The House passed the Affordable Health Care for America Act (H.R. 3962) on November 7 by a 220–215 vote, and the Senate passed the Patient Protection and Affordable Care Act (H.R. 3590) on December 24. Some, however, have expressed doubt that current legislative proposals would significantly reduce the trajectory of health care costs.[69]

A Clean Energy Future

Funding for clean energy investment is contained in the President's Research and Development (R&D) budget request. These initiatives for a new energy economy include reducing U.S. dependence on oil, creating "green" jobs, and reducing the impact of climate change by supporting renewable energy and energy efficiency technologies and limiting carbon emissions and their impact. Additional funding for these initiatives was also contained in ARRA (H.R. 1, P.L. 111-5). The President has proposed the creation of a cap-and-trade system, whereby emission allowances will be auctioned, to provide future funding for these investments.

Education

The President is proposing to increase outlays for education and training with the goal of developing a more skilled and productive labor force. Funding will be provided at both the federal level as well as via grants to state and local governments for individual programs such as Head Start and aid for higher education. Additional outlays for education and training purposes are earmarked for physical investment and research and development.

The federal government also assists individuals and families with the financing of higher education by providing grants, loans, and loan guarantees through various programs. As a result of tight credit markets, Congress enacted legislation to enhance the authority of the Secretary of Education with respect to purchasing student loans made under the Federal Family Education Loan (FFEL) Program and to make other programmatic changes.[70] Building on these reforms, the FY2010 budget proposes to finance future loan originations through the William D. Ford Federal Direct Student Loan Program, generating programmatic savings by eliminating subsidies to FFEL lenders.[71] In addition, the Administration proposes to move Pell Grant outlays from the discretionary spending category to the mandatory spending category. The President also recommends an increase in the maximum award amount for the Pell Grant program. On September 17, 2009, the Student Aid and Fiscal Responsibility Act (H.R. 3221), which incorporates many of the Administration's proposals, passed the House on a 253–171 vote.

Congressional Consideration of the FY2010 Budget Resolution[72]

The House Budget Committee approved its budget resolution (H.Con.Res. 85) on March 25, 2009, on a 24-15 vote. The Senate Budget Committee approved its budget resolution (S.Con.Res. 13) the next day on a 13-10 vote. The House (on a 233-196 vote) and Senate (on a 55-43 vote) agreed to their versions of the budget resolution on April 2, 2009. The conference agreement on the budget resolution (S.Con.Res. 13) was passed in the House (on a 233-193 vote) and in the Senate (on a 53-43 vote) on April 29, 2009.

The House budget resolution provided for revenue levels of $2,328 billion and outlays of $3,550 billion in FY2010, differing slightly from the Senate budget resolution levels of $2,288 billion in revenues and $3,534 billion in outlays. The House budget resolution also included reconciliation instructions to allow for health care and education initiatives, while the Senate did not include any reconciliation instructions. There were some other differences in the House and Senate budget resolutions, including assumptions regarding future legislation concerning estate tax rates and the number of years for which the alternative minimum tax (AMT) would be patched, as well as the number of reserve funds.[73]

A budget resolution conference agreement was filed on April 27, 2009, and included $2,322 billion in revenues and $3,555 billion in outlays for FY2010, resulting in a projected deficit of $1,233 billion. Further, it allowed for $1,086 billion in new, non-war discretionary budget authority, of which $556 billion is allocated for national defense and $530 billion for non-defense discretionary spending. An amount of $130 billion in new budget authority is also provided for overseas deployment and other activities (i.e., war costs). By FY2014, the budget resolution cuts the projected deficit by half to $523 billion. The conference agreement passed both the House and Senate on April 29, 2009.

The conference agreement also assumes three additional years of AMT relief (through FY2014), a two-year extension of expired and expiring tax provisions, and a new incentive for retirement savings. The agreement supports the permanent extension of tax relief first enacted in 2001 and 2003 for middle-income taxpayers (the resolution does assume the expiration of the current top two income tax rates, which will rise to 36 percent and 39.6 percent in 2011) and the continuation of current estate tax rates. The conference agreement does not include any assumptions regarding whether President Obama's Making Work Pay tax credit would be made permanent beyond FY2010.

While legislation addressing these policies is accommodated in the budget resolution conference agreement, such legislation may be constrained by other House and Senate rules, specifically the pay-as-you-go (PAYGO) rules in each chamber (House Rule XXI, clause 10, and Section 201 of S.Con.Res. 21, the FY2008 budget resolution). The budget resolution, however, does provide (in Section 421) that in the House any projected increase in the deficit resulting from certain legislation, relating to the Medicare payment system for physicians, middle class tax relief, reform of the AMT, and reform of the estate and gift tax, up to specified amounts, not count for PAYGO purposes if the House has passed legislation reinstating a statutory PAYGO requirement, or such requirement is in the legislation. The budget resolution conference agreement does not include a similar provision that would apply in the Senate.[74]

President Obama's major initiatives on health care and education reform, clean energy, and infrastructure investment are provided for in separate deficit-neutral reserve funds in the conference agreement. Deficit-neutral reserve funds provide that a committee may report legislation with spending in excess of its allocations, but require the excess amounts be "offset" by equivalent amounts of tax increases or spending cuts.[75]

Reconciliation instructions are also included for health care and education reform initiatives, which directed the committees of jurisdiction in the House and Senate to submit legislative language to their respective Budget Committees by October 15, 2009. Reconciliation instructions are in the form of a directive to a specific committee to recommend legislative changes. These instructions are specific and include (1) the committee responsible for making the change, (2) the dollar amount of the change, and (3) the period over which this change should be measured. Reconciliation instructions also include a deadline for the committee to submit such recommendations. Reconciliation legislation, once reported, is considered under special procedures that limit what matters may be included in reconciliation legislation, prohibit certain amendments, and encourage completion in a timely fashion.[76] The House Education and Labor Committee responded to reconciliation directives by reporting H.R. 3221 on July 21, 2009, and the House Ways and Means Committee responded by reporting H.R. 3200 on October 15, 2009.

Although the overall spending and revenue amounts are enforceable, the policy assumptions underlying the budget resolution are non-binding, leaving Congress and the Administration with some flexibility in making longer-term policy choices.

CONSIDERATIONS FOR CONGRESS

Congress faces extraordinary budgetary challenges in FY2010 with both short-run and long-run budget priorities that may conflict in critical ways. In the short term, economic issues may dominate policy debates, creating pressure for higher deficit spending. In the long term, increasing federal health care costs are expected to keep mandatory spending rising.

Short-Term Considerations

Although estimates for the third quarter of 2009, which put GDP growth at an annual rate of 2.8%, may signal an end to the economic recession, economic conditions remain weak due to budget challenges facing state and local governments, high levels of consumer debt, and continuing weakness in many real estate markets. Most economists expect unemployment rates to remain elevated for the medium term. Congress may choose to enact more government spending in response to the state of the economy. While the power of debt-financed government spending to provide fiscal stimulus is independent of how those funds are spent, clearly taxpayers and beneficiaries of federal programs gain more when that spending reduces households' economic vulnerabilities or promotes future economic efficiency.

Soon after the 111th Congress was sworn in, work began on a major fiscal stimulus package, the American Recovery and Reinvestment Act of 2009 (H.R. 1, P.L. 111-5) , which was enacted February 17, 2009. The $787.2 billion package (according to CBO) includes extended unemployment benefits, aid to state and local governments in the form of higher infrastructure, Medicaid, school spending, health care information technology funding, as well as tax cuts and rebates. The Appendix to this chapter discusses the macroeconomic policy options available to combat economic downturns and details reasons for enacting fiscal stimulus when monetary policy options are no longer available.

Apart from any additional stimulus spending, the U.S. auto industry, facing the worst downturn in auto sales in 15 years and a significant loss in market share, asked for $34 billion in loans through TARP or through other means to revitalize and restructure its companies. The 110th Congress did not pass proposals to provide additional aid to automobile manufacturers in late 2008, but on December 19, 2008, the Bush Administration announced a plan to provide $17.4 billion in loans to General Motors and Chrysler using funds from the Troubled Asset Relief Program (TARP).[77] General Motors and Chrysler have said they would likely have filed for bankruptcy protection if they had failed to receive federal aid. In order to further stabilize the industry, on March 19, 2009, Treasury Secretary Geithner announced a program to provide auto suppliers with up to $5 billion in credit to help ensure the continuation of their operations in the face of slow sales to the struggling auto industry. This program is intended to ensure that suppliers receive payment for their parts shipments regardless of what happens to the downstream car companies. Despite federal aid provided in late 2008 and early 2009, the Chrysler company filed for bankruptcy on April 30, 2009, and General Motors filed for bankruptcy on June 1.[78] On July 10, 2009, a reorganized General Motors emerged from bankruptcy and Chrysler was sold to the Italian car maker Fiat.[79]

General Budget Issues

Congress may wish to consider some general budgeting issues beyond short term considerations of annual funding requests and fiscal stimulus.

ManagingFederalCreditRisks

FCRA requires that federal loan and credit program costs be recorded on a net present value basis. The calculations mandated by FCRA, while an advance over previous practices, do not take into account risks borne by the federal government, and indirectly, risks borne by taxpayers and program beneficiaries. Federal responses to economic and financial turmoil expose the government to substantial credit risks. Congress may opt to consider methods to undertake a systematic accounting of risks undertaken by government activities.

Stimulate and Stop

While some economists contend that sharply rising unemployment rates signal the need for more fiscal stimulus, President Obama said in late June 2009 that a second stimulus package was not yet necessary.[80] In October 2009, however, the President proposed increasing Social Security benefits by $250 for most beneficiaries.

Debt-financed fiscal stimulus measures, like ARRA, eventually must be paid for through higher taxes or future cuts in government programs. Banks and other financial institutions must eventually be weaned off Federal Reserve and Treasury borrowing facilities. After the economic recovery begins, Congress may use oversight authority to rein in spending as soon as is appropriate.

Budget Transparency

The budget, reflecting the size and complexity of the federal government, is complicated and detailed. The budget books that OMB compiles provide an enormous amount of information, and other budget data reported by federal agencies provide even more detail on federal spending plans. The Federal Funding Accountability and Transparency Act of 2006 (P.L. 109-282) included several measures to increase the accessibility of budget information. For example, as a result of that act, OMB now runs the USAspending.gov website, which provides detailed information on federal spending. Some, however, have raised concerns about quality of those data. Moreover, it is not clear that those data are thoroughly coordinated with other federal budgeting data systems.

Congress and the President have undertaken additional efforts in an attempt to improve transparency in light of the large amounts of spending currently occurring as a result of economic stabilization efforts and federal financial interventions. Websites, such as Recovery.gov, were launched to track stimulus spending. The Congressional Oversight Panel was established in EESA to oversee TARP spending. Despite this, criticisms remain and requests for greater transparency continue.

In certain cases, despite the large amount of data provided by OMB and other government agencies, it can be difficult to answer relatively simple budget questions. Critics maintain that the federal government in general and OMB in particular should take steps to make data on federal spending more transparent to taxpayers and more useful to policymakers. Congress may consider requiring these changes to provide more organized and transparent budget data to citizens and to itself.

Budget EnforcementMeasures

The Budget Enforcement Act and other budget enforcement legislation was widely credited for laying the groundwork for the federal government's surpluses in the late 1990s. The Budget Enforcement Act, which imposed certain "Pay-as-you-go" (PAYGO) rules, expired in 2002. PAYGO rules discourage or prevent the enactment of mandatory spending and revenue legislation that is not deficit neutral (i.e., legislation that would cause, or increase, a deficit or reduce a surplus).[81] The House and Senate in the 111th Congress have enacted modified forms of PAYGO procedures. In June 2009, President Obama encouraged Congress to reinstitute statutory PAYGO rules.[82]

When the economy starts to grow again, attention may turn to deficit reduction efforts, in which case PAYGO procedures could become more important. Some budget experts, however, warn that while PAYGO rules in the past have helped enforce stricter budgetary discipline, PAYGO is not a cure-all for fiscal challenges.[83]

Long-Term Considerations

Annual budget deficits or surpluses are not always the best indication of long-term fiscal stability. Most economists agree that, under certain conditions, running a budget deficit may be necessary to provide economic stimulus or pull an economy out of recession. A large budget deficit, in itself, does not necessarily indicate a longer term problem. The federal government, however, faces serious long-term budget challenges. Some measures of fiscal solvency in the long term indicate that the U.S. may face a major future crisis, specifically as it relates to rising healthcare costs and the likely impact on government financed health care spending.

CBO, GAO, and OMB agree that the current mix of federal fiscal policies is unsustainable in the long term. The nation's aging population, combined with rising health care costs per beneficiary, seems likely to keep federal health costs rising faster than per capita GDP. CBO has concluded that "under any plausible scenario, the federal budget is on an unsustainable path," extending well into this century. In their August 2009 budget reports, OMB and CBO identified fiscal challenges related to future healthcare costs as a major issue affecting the country's long-term budget outlook.

Keeping future federal outlays at 20% of GDP, approximately its current share, and leaving fiscal policies unchanged, according to CBO projections, would require drastic reductions in all spending other than that for Medicare, Social Security, and Medicaid or reigning in the costs of these programs. A former CBO Acting Director stated that, "by 2030 ... spending for those programs [Medicare, Social Security, and Medicaid] is projected to reach roughly 15 percent of GDP.... If that increase happened ..., the rest of the budget would have to be cut by more than half" to keep overall spending close to its current level.

The Social Security, Medicare, and Medicaid programs present different challenges to the long-term fiscal position of the federal government. Estimates of the long-term fiscal gap between Social Security (OASDI) outlays and Social Security revenues as a proportion of long-term GDP are generally much smaller than estimates of the long-term fiscal gap between Medicare (HI, Part B, and Part D) outlays and revenues as a portion of long-term GDP. These long-term estimates of fiscal imbalances are sensitive to changes in assumptions regarding productivity growth and interest rates. Spending projections for Medicare and Medicaid are sensitive to medical inflation. Past projections that medical inflation would slow have proved to be overly optimistic.

The call for health care reform has grown. The Obama Administration laid out a reserve fund in their FY2010 budget intended as a down payment to fund future health care reform. The FY2010 budget conference agreement also contained provisions to allow for health care reform legislation. Both House Speaker Pelosi and Senate Majority Leader Reid had indicated that they intended to pass health care reforms in 2009. While the House passed the Affordable Health Care for America Act (H.R. 3962) on November 7 by a 220–215 vote, and the Senate passed the Patient Protection and Affordable Care Act (H.R. 3590) on December 24, it appears that Congress will continue to consider health care reform into 2010.

When the economy recovers, Congress may focus more effort on balancing the budget and reining in the debt. This would require less spending, increases in revenue collections, faster than average economic growth, or a combination of these things. Many economists agree that having some federal debt is a good thing because it builds credit which allows for more favorable borrowing terms. It encourages investment within the country because federal debt is seen as relatively low-risk and safe. Debt is not free, however, and requires interest payments that strain budgets. High debt levels could limit the government's flexibility in meeting its obligations or in responding to emerging needs of its citizens. Ultimately, failing to take action to reduce the projected growth in the debt potentially might lead to future insolvency or government default.[84]

APPENDIX. THE BUDGET AND MACROECONOMIC POLICY

Governments typically strive to keep economic growth steady and employment high while maintaining price stability.[85] Macroeconomic policy instruments are often divided into three components: monetary policy (i.e., control of monetary base and short-term interest rates), fiscal policy (government borrowing and spending), and structural factors. Structural factors include regulation and competition policies that may enhance the efficiency of an economy. While these standard macroeconomic policy tools have been highly effective in moderating economic fluctuations over the past few decades, the financial turmoil and credit crunch in FY2009 present special challenges that led the government to consider other types of responses.

The Limits of Monetary Policy

Monetary policy has several important advantages in macroeconomic stabilization. The Federal Reserve, the central bank of the United States, can deploy traditional monetary policy tools such as open-market interventions that help control certain key short-term federal interest rates. The independence of the Fed insulates it from political pressures and allows it to act quickly in response to new developments in the economy. The Fed, in conjunction with the Treasury Department, developed innovative responses to the financial turmoil that broke out in August 2007. As economic problems deepened in 2008, the Fed redoubled its efforts to unfreeze critical areas of credit markets.

In the current economic situation, traditional monetary policy initiatives appear to have neared their effective limits.[86] In their December meeting, the Federal Reserve set a target range for the federal funds rate between zero and ¼ % and cut the rate on discount window loans (made to commercial banks and other financial institutions) by 75 basis points to ½ %.[87] Thus, the Federal Reserve has little room for further cuts. In addition, declining investment demand and investors seeking a safe harbor for funds have pushed short-term interest rates on federal Treasury securities to very low levels.

Furthermore, many economists doubt that pushing those interest rates even lower would spur much additional lending when banks and other lenders worry about the solvency of financial counterparties. Monetary policy loses much of its effectiveness in such a "liquidity trap," as banks' reluctance to lend frustrates the Fed's efforts to expand the money supply. Moreover, while new Federal Reserve lending facilities may improve credit conditions or at least limit further deterioration, those programs were not designed to address the larger macroeconomic issue of stimulating economic growth.[88] Finally, while the Fed responses in 2008 and early 2009 have been aggressive and creative, there may be limits to what additional programs can accomplish.

Logic of Fiscal Stimulus

The context for fiscal policy begins with national income accounting. The national income, as measured by GDP, is the sum of expenditure categories. Specifically, the national income accounting identity is

$$Y \equiv C + I + G + \text{Net Exports}$$

where
Y = national income (GDP)
C = private consumption
I = private investment
G = government spending.

The identity implies that national income falls when private consumption and investment fall unless offset by increases in either government spending or net exports. In the current economic environment, government spending increases have become the focus of attention as a source of stimulus as consumption and investment continue to decline. While some measures of economic activity remained resilient in the first half of 2008, despite rapidly rising unemployment and sharp drops in asset prices and in housing prices in many areas of the country, most forecasters predict sharp decreases in key economic indicators in 2009.[89]

Private consumption fell in the last half of 2008 for several reasons. Rising unemployment rates left some households with lost earnings, and prompted others to increase savings to cushion against possible future job losses. Some households that had borrowed using home equity credit lines, credit cards, or other types of credit became unable to continue borrowing, thus requiring cutbacks in consumption. Other households became unable to afford mortgage payments, contributing to increasing foreclosure rates and reducing consumption. Auto sales, an important component of private consumption, fell drastically as financing became harder to obtain and gas prices rose in mid-2008.

Private investment falls when businesses believe that demand for what they sell is falling or will fall. Non-residential investment, a component of private investment, has been weak relative to historical levels since the mid-1990s, although information technology investment was strong until the collapse of dot-coms in 2000. The Federal Reserve then sharply lowered short-term interest rates. Capital inflows, especially from East Asia, pushed down market interest rates. Low interest rates helped housing prices rise and stimulated new residential construction and development, boosting fixed residential investment.

As housing prices in many areas of the country reached their peak or began to decline in 2007, investors who once had thought that home prices would continue to rise backed away. Additionally, many investors began to fear that residential mortgage-backed securities (RMBS) were much riskier than anticipated, and capital markets became reluctant to put more money into the residential sector. A credit crunch, partially sparked by concerns over RMBS, emerged in August 2007. Foreclosure rates have climbed, as refinancing options for many homeowners dwindled, putting added downward pressure on home prices. High levels of fixed residential investment over the past decade have created large inventories of new houses, which may dampen incentives for future construction. All of these variables contributed to declines in private investment, which are not expected to reverse in the near term.

The United States has run trade deficits since the mid-1980s. In recent years, the trade deficit has narrowed (so that net exports are less negative) in part because the dollar has weakened relative to most major currencies. Sharply higher energy prices in 2008 offset many of those gains, but falling energy prices in late 2008 may help shrink the trade deficit further. As trading partners have begun to face their own economic problems, demand for American exports may fall. American consumers, however, may buy fewer imported goods during the recession. The combined effect on net exports is likely to be mixed, causing them to be an ineffective source of stimulus.

Most macroeconomists believe that reductions in private consumption and investment will cut economic growth unless debt-financed government spending increases to provide substantial fiscal stimulus. Other measures, such as investment incentives or broad tax cuts may also promote economic growth, although some economists believe debt-financed government spending is a more effective stimulus to aggregate demand in a recession.

Applying Fiscal Policy

Standard applied macroeconomic theory suggests that fiscal policy is more effective when short-term interest rates are extremely low. Fiscal policy therefore plays an especially important role in economic policy during economic downturns. The amount and composition of the federal spending along with the size of the federal deficit are key fiscal policy instruments.

During economic downturns, government revenues fall and expenditures rise as more people become eligible for unemployment insurance and income support programs, causing deficits to increase or surpluses to shrink. These effects, known as "automatic stabilizers," provide a countercyclical stimulus in the short run without the need for new legislative action. Automatic stabilizers, however, probably cannot provide enough fiscal stimulus to pull the current economy out of a recession.

Higher government spending financed by borrowing, above and beyond the automatic stabilizer effects, provides a powerful fiscal policy tool that can help counteract recessions. A countercyclical fiscal policy, in which taxes are cut or spending is increased, can dampen economic fluctuations and limit the depth of economic downturns.

Debt-financed government spending is one component of Keynesian demand management—the theory that government can stabilize the economy, or at least moderate economic fluctuations by using fiscal policy to offset changes in private consumption and investment. The federal government, according to that theory, can shift buying power from future to the present more easily than firms and households, and is therefore better able to maintain stable economic conditions. In the view of most macroeconomists, Keynesian demand management, as one component of a well-designed macroeconomic policy regime, can increase economic efficiency by preventing labor and capital goods from becoming unnecessarily idle during economic downturns.

Reducing government deficits when economic growth is robust is another key component of a well-designed macroeconomic policy regime. In this respect, responsible fiscal policy requires that spending in economic downturns be paid for by future spending reductions and/or tax increases. Of course, higher taxes in the future reduce private consumption and cuts in future government programs reduce consumption of publicly provided goods and services. If debt is not reduced, higher interest rates may reduce future investment.

CaveatsRegarding Fiscal Stimulus

Some economists have criticized the logic of Keynesian demand management and the discretionary application of fiscal spending by governments. Some have contended that Keynesian fiscal policy arguments do not take sufficient account of choices made by firms and individual households. Others argue that Keynesian demand management policies can create administrative problems and note that mustering the political will to maintain a sustainable fiscal policy by reducing spending over the economic cycle can be hard.

Some economists have argued that not just the government, but also households can shift spending through time via borrowing and saving. Thus households, according to some, may counteract government fiscal policies by saving during economic downturns, thus further reducing consumption. Other economists note that many households are not in a position to choose between saving and consuming and that the low interest rates typically found in economic downturns may weaken incentives to save. Some evidence suggests that high-income households may take savings measures that offset government fiscal policies, but low-income households are, in general, less able to rearrange their finances in ways that would reduce the effectiveness of fiscal policy.

The argument for Keynesian demand management presumes that governments run surpluses during economic expansions to repay debt accumulated when applying fiscal stimulus during economic downturns. Critics of deficit-financed fiscal policy argue that policymakers are more willing to raise government spending when economic growth slows than to cut spending when growth accelerates.[90] Certain federal programs or increased spending, enacted during economic downturns, may remain in place after they are no longer necessary because of the interests of influential beneficiaries rather than overall economic welfare. On the other hand, some programs created during the Great Depression such as Social Security, have helped make many families less vulnerable to economic shocks.

Few economists believe that large changes in fiscal policy designed to counterbalance short-term economic downturns can be timed precisely. Certainly, macroeconomists are more skeptical about the ability to fine-tune fiscal policy than their predecessors a generation ago. Most macroeconomists nonetheless believe fiscal policy is an important tool during deep or prolonged periods of slow or negative growth.

End Notes

[1]For more information, see CRS Report 98-721, *Introduction to the Federal Budget Process*, by Robert Keith.

[2] U.S. Department of Commerce, Bureau of Economic Analysis, "Gross Domestic Product: Third Quarter 2009 (2nd Estimate)," press release BEA 09-50, November 24, 2009, available at http://bea.gov/newsreleases/national/gdp/2009/ pdf/gdp3q09_2nd.pdf.

[3]U.S. Congressional Budget Office, *The Budget and Economic Outlook: An Update,* August 2009, Table 2-1.

[4] U.S. Congressional Budget Office, *A Preliminary Analysis of the President's Budget and an Update of CBO's Budget and Economic Outlook*, March 2009, available at http://www.cbo.gov/ftpdocs/100xx/doc10014/03-20-PresidentBudget.pdf. Older data were taken from Office of Management and Budget (OMB) historical statistics.

[5] Most economists use data on federal outlays to track larger budget trends, while most program analysts use budget authority to track changes in specific program areas.

[6] Press Release from Timothy Geithner, Secretary of the Treasury, and Peter Orszag, Director of the Office of Management and Budget, *Budget Results for Fiscal Year 2009,* October 16, 2009, available at http://www.treas.gov/ press/releases/tg322.htm.

[7] U.S. Office of Management and Budget, *Budget for Fiscal Year 2010, Mid-Session Review*, Table S-1, August 2009, http://www.whitehouse.gov/omb/budget/MSR/; "A New Era of Responsibility: Renewing America's Promise," February 26, 2009. A detailed discussion of how the FY2009 deficit has changed since the estimates were last issued is provided later in this chapter, in the section titled, "Why Did Budget Deficit Estimates for FY2009 Change?"

[8]Stan Collender, "2009 Deficit: I'm Telling You For The Last Time ... ," *Roll Call*, September 13, 2009.

[9] Ibid, pp. 25-27, and Testimony of Elizabeth Warren, Chair of the Congressional Oversight Panel, in Congress, Senate Banking Committee, *Pulling Back the TARP: Oversight of the Financial Rescue Program*, hearings, 111th Congress, 1st sess., February 5, 2009, available at http://banking.senate.gov/public/_files/Warrentestimonyfinal2509.pdf.

[10] For more information on trends in discretionary and mandatory spending, see CRS Report RL34424, *Trends in Discretionary Spending*, by D. Andrew Austin and Mindy R. Levit and CRS Report RL33074, *Mandatory Spending Since 1962*, by D. Andrew Austin and Mindy R. Levit.

[11] U.S. Congressional Budget Office, *The Budget and Economic Outlook: An Update*, August 2009, available at http://www.cbo.gov/doc.cfm?index=10521.

[12] For more information see CRS Report RS20129, *Entitlements and Appropriated Entitlements in the Federal Budget Process*, by Bill Heniff Jr.

[13] U.S. Department of the Treasury, "Joint Statement of Tim Geithner, Secretary of the Treasury, and Peter Orszag, Director of the Office of Management and Budget, on Budget Results for Fiscal Year 2009," Press release TG-322, October 16, 2009, available at *http://www.t* reas.gov/press/releases/tg322.htm.

[14]See CRS Report RL33623, *Long-Term Measures of Fiscal Imbalance*, by D. Andrew Austin.

[15]Committee for a Responsible Federal Budget, *Good Deficit / Bad Deficit*, April 2009.

[16] U.S. Office of Management and Budget, *Budget for Fiscal Year 2009*, *Historical Tables*, Table 1-3, available at http://www.gpoaccess.gov/usbudget/fy09/pdf/hist.pdf.

[17] Gross federal debt is also referred to as total debt or total public debt outstanding. Intragovernmental debt is also referred to as intragovernmental holdings or debt held by federal government accounts.

[18] U.S. Office of Management and Budget, *Budget of the U.S. Government, Fiscal Year 2009, Analytical Perspectives*, Feb. 2008, p. 408.

[19]For more information, see CRS Report RL34712, *Ebbs and Flows of Federal Debt*, by Mindy R. Levit.

[20] General Accountability Office, *Debt Ceiling: Analysis of Actions Taken During the 2003 Debt Issuance Suspension Period*, GAO-04-526, May 20, 2004.

[21]U.S. Congressional Budget Office, *The Budget and Economic Outlook: An Update*, August 2009, p. 21.

[22] David Clarke, "Treasury Gives Congress More Breathing Room on Debt Limit," *CQ Today Online News – Budget*, Nov. 4, 2009; U.S. Treasury Department, "November 2009 Quarterly Refunding Statement," Press release TG346, November 4, 2009.

[23] For further details, see CRS Report RL31967, *The Debt Limit: History and Recent Increases*, by D. Andrew Austin and Mindy R. Levit.

[24]Ibid., Table 1-2.

[25] Carmen M. Reinhart and Kenneth S. Rogoff, "The Aftermath of Financial Crises," *American Economic Review*, vol. 99 (2009), no. 2; Alan Auerbach and William Gale, "The Economic Crisis and the Fiscal Crisis: 2009 and Beyond," Tax Policy Center working paper, February 2009, available at http://www.taxpolicycenter.org/UploadedPDF/ 411843_ economic _crisis.pdf.

[26]CRS Report 98-325, *The Federal Fiscal Year*, by Bill Heniff Jr.

[27]The contents of the Presidential budget submission are governed by U.S. Code, Title 31, Sec. 1105.

[28] Additional information on budget during transition is available in CRS Report RS20752, *Submission of the President's Budget in Transition Years*, by Robert Keith.

[29] U.S. Congressional Budget Office, *Estimated Impact on the Deficit of Three Alternative Policy Scenarios as Specified by Speaker Pelosi and Chairman Spratt*, February 23, 2009, available at http://www.cbo.gov/ftpdocs/100xx/ doc10003/02-23-ThreePolicyScenarios.pdf and *Estimated Macroeconomic Impacts of the American Recovery and Reinvestment Act of 2009*, March 2, 2009, available at http://www.cbo.gov/ftpdocs/100xx/doc10008/03-02-Macro_Effects_of_ARRA.pdf.

[30] U.S. Congressional Budget Office, *A Preliminary Analysis of the President's Budget and an Update of CBO's Budget and Economic Outlook*, March 2009.

[31] U.S. Congressional Budget Office, *An Analysis of the President's Budgetary Proposals for Fiscal Year 2010*, June 2009.

[32] U.S. Congressional Budget Office, *The Budget and Economic Outlook: An Update,* August 2009, http://www.cbo.gov/ftpdocs/105xx/doc10521/08-25-BudgetUpdate.pdf.

[33] While some budget enforcement legislation constraining the computation of CBO baseline estimates has expired, CBO has continued to follow those legislative guidelines.

[34]CRS Report R40438, *Ongoing Government Assistance for American International Group (AIG)*, by Baird Webel.

[35] For a detailed chronology, see the St. Louis Federal Reserve Bank, *The Financial Crisis: A Timeline of Events and Policy Actions*, available at *http://timeline.* stlouisfed.org/ index.cfm?p=timeline#2008-10.

[36] Blue Chip Economic Indicators, "Top Analysts' Forecast of the U.S. Economic Outlook for the Year Ahead," press release, November 10, 2009, available at http://www.bluechippubs.com.

[37]U.S. Congressional Budget Office, *The Budget and Economic Outlook: An Update,* August 2009, Table 2-1.

[38] For more information, see CRS Report RL34730, *Troubled Asset Relief Program: Legislation and Treasury Implementation*, by Baird Webel and Edward V. Murphy.

[39] U.S. Department of Treasury, "Treasury Department Announces Initial Closings of Legacy Securities Public-Private Investment Funds," press release, September 30, 2009, http://www.ustreas.gov; Maya Jackson Randall and Jeff Bater, "Update: US Govt Announces Investment In Toxic-Asset Program," *Wall Street Journal*, November 3, 2009.

[40] U.S. Congressional Budget Office, *Cost Estimate For the Conference Agreement For H.R. 1.*, February 13, 2009, available at http://cbo.gov/ftpdocs/99xx/doc9989/hr1conference.pdf.

[41] For more information on the provisions of ARRA, see CRS Report R40537, *American Recovery and Reinvestment Act of 2009 (P.L. 111-5): Summary and Legislative History*, by Clinton T. Brass et al.

[42]Mandated by Section 123 of the Emergency Economic Stabilization Act (P.L. 110-343).

[43]U.S. Office of Management and Budget, *Budget for Fiscal Year 2010, Mid-Session Review*, Table S-4.

[44]U.S. Congressional Budget Office, *The Budget and Economic Outlook: An Update*, Table 1-4.

[45] President Obama's budget documents for FY2010 included an additional $250 billion as a placeholder for potential future financial stabilization efforts in FY2009. However, in its Mid-Session Review, OMB removed this placeholder.

[46] The Federal Credit Reform Act of 1990 was created as part of the Omnibus Budget Reconciliation Act of 1990 (P.L. 101-508). FCRA defines a subsidy cost as "the estimated long-term cost to the government of a direct loan or a loan guarantee, calculated on a net present value basis, excluding administrative costs." For details, see CRS Report RL30346, *Federal Credit Reform: Implementation of the Changed Budgetary Treatment of Direct Loans and Loan Guarantees*, by James M. Bickley.

[47] While the FCRA calculations include estimates of default costs, they do not discount more volatile income flows, as a private firm would.

[48] U.S. Congressional Budget Office, *Estimating the Value of Subsidies for Federal Loans and Loan Guarantees*, Aug. 2004, available at http://cbo.gov/doc.cfm?index=5751.

[49] U.S. Congressional Budget Office, *The Budget and Economic Outlook: Fiscal Years 2009 to 2019*, January 7, 2009, pp. 25-26, available at *http://www.* cbo.gov/ ftpdocs/99xx/doc9957 /01-07-Outlook.pdf; Testimony of Elizabeth Warren, Chair of the Congressional Oversight Panel, in Congress, Senate Banking Committee, *Pulling Back the TARP: Oversight of the Financial Rescue Program*, hearings, 111th Congress, 1st sess., February 5, 2009, available at http://banking.senate.gov/ public/_files/ Warrentestimonyfinal2509.pdf.

[50] U.S. government is widely regarded as having no default risk, although government securities may carry other risks, such as interest rate risks and for foreign holders, exchange rate risks.

[51] U.S. Congressional Budget Office, *Estimating the Value of Subsidies for Federal Loans and Loan Guarantees*, Aug. 2004, p. 4.

[52]For details, see CRS Report RL34427, *Financial Turmoil: Federal Reserve Policy Responses*, by Marc Labonte.

[53] The Congressional Budget Act sets April 15 as a target date for Congress to adopt a budget resolution. In some years, that target date was not met. For more information see CRS Report 98-814, *Budget Reconciliation Legislation: Development and Consideration*, by Bill Heniff Jr.

[54] Section written by Amy Belasco, CRS.

[55] CRS Report RS22455, *Military Operations: Precedents for Funding Contingency Operations in Regular or in Supplemental Appropriations Bills*, by Stephen Daggett, pp. 5-6. For a discussion of how war funding may affect the federal budget, see CRS Report RL31176, *Financing Issues and Economic Effects of American Wars*, by Marc Labonte and Mindy R. Levit.

[56] CRS Report RL33110, *The Cost of Iraq, Afghanistan, and Other Global War on Terror Operations Since 9/11*, by Amy Belasco.

[57] Office of Management and Budget, "Letter to the President on the FY2009 Supplemental," Estimate No. 1, 111th Congress, April 9, 2009, available at http://www.cq.com/flatfiles/editorialFiles/temporaryItems/2009/supp-omb-letter.pdf; Office of Management and Budget, FY2009 Supplemental Request, Estimate No.1, 111th Congress, April 9, 2009, available at http://www.whitehouse.gov/omb/assets/budget_amendments/supplemental_04_09_09.pdf.

[58] OMB, *A New Era of Responsibility: Renewing America's Promise*, February 26, 2009, pp. 53-55 and Table S-7; "Responsibly Ending the War in Iraq," Remarks by President Barack Obama at Camp Lejeune, North Carolina, February 27, 2009, available at http://www.whitehouse.gov/the_press_office/Remarks-of-President-Barack-Obama-Responsibly-Ending-the-War-in-Iraq/; White House, Blog, "A New Strategy for Afghanistan and Pakistan, March 27, 2009, available at *http://www.whitehouse.go* v/blog/09/03/27/A-New-Strategy-for-Afghanistan-and-Pakistan/.

[59] *Congressional Record*, "Supplemental Appropriations Act 2009 (H.R. 2346) Conference Agreement (H.Rept. 111-151), June 16, 2009, pp. H6871-H6905; see also CRS Report R40531, *FY2009 Spring Supplemental Appropriations for Overseas Contingency Operations*, coordinated by Stephen Daggett and Susan B. Epstein.

[60] For further details on the program, see CRS Report R40654, *Accelerated Vehicle Retirement for Fuel Economy: "Cash for Clunkers,"* by Brent D. Yacobucci and Bill Canis.

[61] U.S. Congressional Budget Office, *The Budget and Economic Outlook: An Update*, Table A-1. Further details explaining the changes in the baseline deficit estimates between March and August are explained in Appendix A of that report.

[62] U.S. Office of Management and Budget, *Budget for Fiscal Year 2010, Mid-Session Review*, Table 1, p. 2, and p. 15.

[63] For details on the progress of appropriations bills, see the CRS Appropriations Status Table, available at http://crs.gov/products/appropriations/appover.shtml. The Congressional Budget Office's "Discretionary Appropriations Status Tables" are available at http://www.cbo.gov/budget/approps.shtml.

[64] *A New Era of Responsibility: Renewing America's Promise* is the budget overview document released in February. The summary tables in this document were updated in May in the publication titled *Updated Summary Tables*. The other four volumes were released in May. The President's budget proposals can be found on the OMB website at http://www.whitehouse.gov/omb/budget/.

[65] For details of these projections, see U.S. Office of Management and Budget, *Budget for Fiscal Year 2010, Mid-Session Review*, Tables S-1 (Proposed Budget) and S-7 (BEA Baseline and Current Policy).

[66] The tax cuts were enacted in the Economic Growth and Taxpayer Relief Act of 2001 (EGTRRA; P.L. 107-16) and the Jobs and Growth Tax Relief Reconciliation Act of 2003 (JGTRRA; P.L. 108-27).

[67] For a discussion of budgetary enforcement legislation, see CRS Report 98-721, *Introduction to the Federal Budget Process*, by Robert Keith.

[68] For more details, see CRS Report R40581, *Health Reform and the 111th Congress*, by HindaChaikind; and CRS Report R40517, *Health Care Reform: An Introduction*, coordinated by Bernadette Fernandez.

[69]Ceci Connolly, "Health Bills Too Timid On Cutting Costs, Experts Say," *Washington Post*, November 4, 2009, p. A1.

[70] For more information on recent Congressional action regarding these programs, see CRS Report RL34452, *The Ensuring Continued Access to Student Loans Act of 2008*, by David P. Smole.

[71] For more information on the FFEL and William D. Ford Federal Direct Student Loan Program, see CRS Report R40122, *Federal Student Loans Made Under the Federal Family Education Loan Program and the William D. Ford Federal Direct Loan Program: Terms and Conditions for Borrowers*, by David P. Smole.

[72] For more information on consideration and the policies of the Congressional Budget Resolution, see CRS Report R40559, *S.Con.Res. 13: The Budget Resolution for FY2010*, by Megan Suzanne Lynch and Mindy R. Levit.

[73] Details of the House-passed budget resolution are available at *http://budget.* house. gov/menu_congress.shtml. Details of the Senate-passed budget resolution are available at http://budget.senate.gov/democratic/senatebudres.html.

[74] For more information on PAYGO requirements, see CRS Report RL34300, *Pay-As-You-Go Procedures for Budget Enforcement*, by Robert Keith.

[75] For more information on reserve funds, see CRS Report R40472, *The Budget Resolution and Spending Legislation*, by Megan Suzanne Lynch.

[76] For more information on reconciliation legislation, see CRS Report 98-814, *Budget Reconciliation Legislation: Development and Consideration*, by Bill Heniff Jr.

[77] John D. McKinnon and John D. Stoll, "U.S. Throws Lifeline to Detroit," *Wall Street Journal*, December 20, 2008; U.S. Department of Treasury, "Secretary Paulson Statement on Stabilizing the Automotive Industry," Press release HP-1332, December 19, 2008, available at http://www.ustreas.gov/press/releases/hp1332.htm.

[78] See CRS Report R40003, *U.S. Motor Vehicle Industry: Federal Financial Assistance and Restructuring*, coordinated by Bill Canis.

[79]Micheline Maynard, "A Primer on the New General Motors," *New York Times*, July 10, 2009; Michael J. De La Merced And Micheline Maynard, "Fiat Deal With Chrysler Seals Swift 42-Day Overhaul," *New York Times*, June 11, 2009, p. B4.

[80]*New York Times*, "President Obama's Press Briefing," June 23, 2009, available at http://www.nytimes.com/2009/06/ 23/us/politics/23text-obama.htm.

[81]See CRS Report RL34300, *Pay-As-You-Go Procedures for Budget Enforcement*, by Robert Keith.

[82] White House, "President Obama Calls for Restoring Statutory Pay-As-You-Go Requirements," press release, June 9, 2009, available at *http://www.whitehouse.gov/the_pre* ss_office/President-Obama-Calls-for-Restoring-Statutory-Pay-As-You-Go-Requirements/.

[83]Stan Collender, "PAYGO Is Just a Condiment, Not the Main Ingredient," *Roll Call*, June 23, 2009.

[84] Recent trends in the credit default swap market imply an increased market perception of the likelihood of default on certain Treasury securities. In past years, Treasury securities were typically regarded as risk-free. See Alan Auerbach and William Gale, "The Economic Crisis and the Fiscal Crisis: 2009 and Beyond: An Update," Tax Policy Center working paper, September 2009, available at http://www.brookings.edu/~/media/Files/rc/papers/2009/ 06_fiscal_crisis_gale/06_fiscal_crisis_gale_update.pdf.

[85] The Humphrey-Hawkins Act (P.L. 95-523) specifies price stability and full employment as goals of national economic policy. Most economists interpret full employment to mean the highest level of employment consistent with a sustainable macroeconomic policy. See John. P. Judd and Glenn D. Rudebusch, "The Goals of U.S. Monetary Policy," *FRBSF Economic Letter* 99-04, January 29, 1999, available at http://www.frbsf.org/econrsrch/wklyltr/ wklyltr99/el99-04.html.

[86] For example, Jan Hatzius, Chief Economist for Goldman Sachs's U.S. Research Department, wrote that "with riskless short-term interest rates now close to zero, conventional monetary

policy is becoming ineffective." "Macro Policy in a Liquidity Trap," *US Economics Analyst*, issue 08/46, November 14, 2008.

[87] Federal Reserve Bank Board of Governors, Press Release, December 16, 2008, available at http://www.federalreserve.gov/newsevents/press/monetary/20081216b.htm.

[88] These credit facilities, according to the Federal Reserve, were created to increase the availability of credit and to reduce interest rate spreads to more normal levels. While these facilities have greatly expanded the Federal Reserve's balance sheet, they do not appear to have had significant effects on monetary aggregates. See "Term Asset-Backed Securities Loan Facility: Frequently Asked Questions," December 19, 2008, available at http://www.newyorkfed.org// markets/talf_faq.html.

[89] For example, the December 2008 Blue Chip Consensus Forecast, compiled from predictions of 50 economists, foresees a 1.1% decline in real GDP. Blue Chip Economic Indicators, *Top Analysts' Forecasts of the U.S. Economic Outlook for the Year Ahead*, vol. 33, no. 12, December 10, 2008. Most of the forecasters surveyed by Blue Chip based their predictions on the presumption that Congress will pass a major fiscal stimulus package. The January 2009 CBO baseline, which does not presume a fiscal stimulus package will pass, projects a 2.2% decline in GDP in FY2009. U.S. Congressional Budget Office, *The Budget and Economic Outlook: Fiscal Years 2009 to 2019*, January 7, 2009, available at http://www.cbo.gov/ftpdocs/99xx/doc9957/01-07-Outlook.pdf.

[90] Milton Friedman, *Capitalism and Freedom* (Chicago: Univ. of Chicago Press, 1962), pp. 75-84.

In: Federal Budget Outlook and Economic... ISBN: 978-1-61761-769-0
Editors: Michael S. Okada

Chapter 2

THE ECONOMIC IMPLICATIONS OF THE LONG-TERM FEDERAL BUDGET OUTLOOK

Marc Labonte

SUMMARY

Following the financial crisis, the budget deficit reached 10% of GDP in 2009, a level that cannot be sustained in the long run. Concerns about long-term fiscal sustainability depend on the projected future path of the budget, absent future policy changes. The retirement of the baby boomers, rising life expectancy, and the rising cost of medical care result in projections of large and growing budget deficits over the next several decades. Social Security outlays are projected to rise from 4.8% of gross domestic product (GDP) today to 6.0% of GDP in 2035, and Medicare and Medicaid outlays are projected to rise from 5.3% today to as much as 10.0% of GDP in 2035 and 12.7% of GDP in 2050. These increases in spending are not expected to subside after the baby boomers have passed away. Without any corresponding rise in revenues, this spending path would lead to unsustainably large and persistent budget deficits, which would push up interest rates and the trade deficit, crowd out private investment spending, and ultimately cause fiscal crisis.

To avoid this outcome, taxes would need to be raised or expenditures would need to be reduced. Altering taxes and benefits ahead of time would reduce the size of adjustments required in the future, if the proceeds were used to increase national saving. (Making changes ahead of time would also allow individuals time to adjust their private saving behavior.) National saving can be increased by using the proceeds to pay down the national debt, purchase financial securities, or finance individual accounts. But if the budget savings is offset by new spending or tax cuts, the government's ability to finance future benefits will not have improved. Individual accounts financed by increasing the budget deficit, however, would not increase national saving or reduce the government's fiscal imbalance and could exacerbate the government's fiscal imbalance over the 75-year projection.

Relatively small tax increases or benefit reductions could return Social Security to long-run solvency. Restraining the growth in Medicare and Medicaid spending is more uncertain and difficult, however. The projected increase in spending is driven more by medical spending outpacing general spending increases than by demographic change. But it is uncertain how to restrain cost growth because much of it is the result of technological innovation that makes new and expensive treatments available. If future medical spending grows more slowly than projected, then the long-term budget outlook improves dramatically. From a government-wide perspective, Social Security or Medicare trust fund assets cannot help finance future benefits because they are redeemed with general revenues at a time when the overall budget is in deficit.

The reason revenues are not projected to rise along with outlays is that these programs are financed on a pay-as-you-go basis: current workers finance the benefits of current retirees. In the future, there will be fewer workers per retiree. Once a pay-as-you-go system is up and running and faced with an adverse demographic shift, there is no reform that can avoid making some present or future generation receive less than past generations. Under current policy, future generations will be made worse off by higher taxes or lower benefits. Under a reform that increases national saving, some of that burden would be shifted to current generations. Overall, current budget deficits negate the system's limited existing prefunding, exacerbating the future fiscal shortfall. While entitlement spending on the elderly is the major driver behind future deficits, it played little part in the growth of the current budget deficit. Reducing the current deficit is the most straightforward and concrete step that can be taken today to reduce the future shortfall.

The United States is projected to undergo a demographic shift as the aging of the baby boomers causes an unprecedented increase in the fraction of the population that is retired. TCoupled with rising life expectancy, this means, under current policy, a steady increase in the portion of the population that is both out of the workforce and receiving social insurance benefits from the government. At the same time, the cost of health care has persistently outpaced income growth, and may continue to do so while an aging population is utilizing more health care. If left unattended, this situation poses serious challenges for the government's fiscal position and the economy as a whole.[1]

Following the financial crisis, the budget deficit reached 10% of GDP in 2009, a level that cannot be sustained in the long run. Concerns about long-term fiscal sustainability depend on the projected future path of the budget, absent future policy changes. While the recent growth in the budget deficit was due to short-term developments unrelated to entitlement spending on the elderly, the projected path of the budget in the long run primarily depends on the future path of entitlement spending.[2]This chapter analyzes the long-run path of the federal budget; for a discussion of the current fiscal situation, see CRS Report R40770, *Economic Effects of a Budget Deficit Exceeding $1 Trillion*.

PROJECTIONS SHOW THAT CURRENT FISCAL POLICY IS UNSUSTAINABLE

Social Security and Medicare are financed primarily on a pay-as-you-go basis: benefits paid to today's elderly are based on dedicated payroll taxes collected from today's workers.[3]Under current policy, expenditures are projected to grow much more rapidly than revenues because of the increase in retirees relative to workers. The worker to recipient ratio for Social Security is shown in Figure 1 and is projected to fall from 3.2 workers per recipient in 2008 to 2.2 workers per recipient in 2030. (The worker to recipient ratio for Medicare is slightly lower than for Social Security, but exhibits the same pattern over the long-run projection.) The projected decline in the worker to recipient ratio is driven by the retirement of the baby boomers, declining fertility, and increasing life expectancy, which means that, under current policy and retirement patterns, workers will be spending a larger fraction of their lives in retirement (assuming workers' and employers' attitudes toward retirement do not change). Thus, the increases in spending are not projected to subside after the baby boomers have passed away. Worker to recipient forecasts are subject to large margins of uncertainty, represented by the high and low lines in the graph. But even under the most optimistic of assumptions about population growth, the worker to recipient ratio will fall well below historical levels in coming years.

For elderly entitlement spending to keep in line with revenues in light of these demographic changes, some combination of expenditures reduction and revenue increase will be required. Social Security and Medicare are financed through dedicated revenues: the payroll (FICA) tax. As shown below, diverting existing general revenues to entitlement spending cannot realistically cover the financing gap because of the sheer magnitude of the gap relative to total government revenues. Thus, the financing problem should not be thought of as a programmatic problem, but rather as a government-wide problem, and is best analyzed relative to economic output (GDP). (The role of the Social Security and Medicare trust funds will be discussed below.)

Figure 2 illustrates the projected increase in Social Security spending from the present to 2105. Projected spending increases from 4.8% of GDP in 2008 to 5.8% of GDP in 2058, whereas revenues are projected to stay fairly constant as a proportion of GDP. However, there is a high degree of uncertainty surrounding these projections. The Congressional Budget Office (CBO) estimates that there is a 10% chance that spending will exceed 7.0% of GDP by 2058, and a 10% chance that spending will be below 4.9% of GDP that year. By contrast, revenue projections show a very narrow degree of uncertainty as a share of GDP, so that under almost any scenario a large shortfall between revenues and spending is projected.[4]

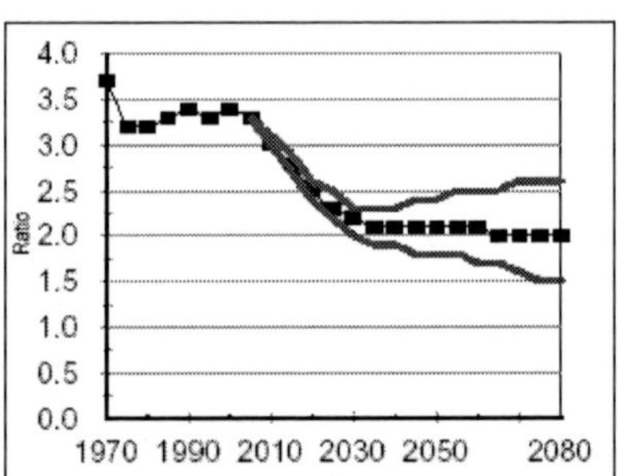

Source: Trustees of OASDI, Annual Report, 2009, Table IV.B2.

Note: Middle line based on Trustees' intermediate assumptions. Outside lines represent worker-recipient ratios under alternative scenarios. Beneficiaries include the retired, survivors, dependents, and the disabled.

Figure 1. Worker to Recipient Ratio for Social Security, 1970-2080

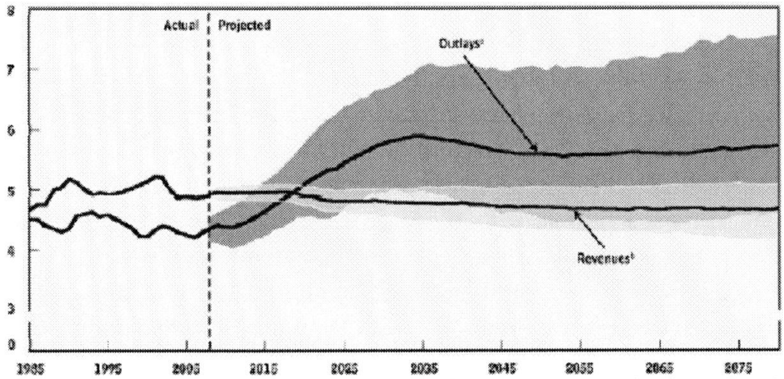

Source: Congressional Budget Office, Updated Long-Term Projections for Social Security, August 2008. Notes: The dark lines indicate CBO's projections of expected outcomes. Shaded areas indicate the 80 percent range of uncertainty around each projection based on a distribution of 500 simulations from CBO's long-term model. (An 80 percent range means that there is a 10 percent chance that actual values will be above that range, a 10 percent chance that they will be below it, and an 80 percent chance that they will fall within the range.) In the scheduled benefits scenario, workers each year receive full benefits as calculated under current law.

a. Includes scheduled benefits and administrative costs.

b. Includes payroll taxes and revenues from the taxation of benefits.

Figure 2. Social Security Spending and Revenues as a % of GDP

Social Security projections are based on straightforward assumptions since benefits are determined by specific rules and formulas and demographic projections. By contrast, there is no obvious way to project Medicare and Medicaid spending into the future because widely differing assumptions can be made about how much will be spent per beneficiary under current law.[5] While there are fairly reliable projections of the number of Medicare beneficiaries, and current law broadly specifies the medical services that Medicare and Medicaid will cover, little can be known about how medical treatments, costs, and technologies will evolve in the future, or what new treatments will become available in the future. New technologies could potentially lower costs through productivity gains, but they could also potentially raise costs by making new treatments available that are both more effective and more expensive.

In recent history, the latter has occurred, and as a result health spending has risen more rapidly than GDP (referred to as *excess cost growth*). However, there is no guarantee that this pattern will continue in the future. In fact, it is unreasonable to extrapolate historical excess cost growth indefinitely, since that would result in health care eventually consuming 100% of GDP.[6] Unfortunately, although there is great uncertainty about what future rate of excess cost growth above growth in GDP per capita is reasonable, Medicare and Medicaidexpenditure projections are highly sensitive to this assumption. To illustrate the sensitivity, Figure 3 compares CBO's projection of Medicare and Medicaid spending to two other scenarios: that the historical growth rates of 2.5% persisted and that excess cost growth is eliminated.[7]

CBO's projection is based on the assumption that excess cost growth will eventually slow down enough to allow non-health consumption to grow modestly (in absolute terms). Specifically, CBO assumes that excess cost growth will slow from 2.3% in 2020 to 0.9% in 2083 for Medicare and from 1.9% in 2020 to 0.1% in 2083 for Medicaid. (Medicaid cost growth slows more because, although CBO cannot assume that current federal policy can change, it can assume that state policy would change, and Medicaid is a jointly financed federal-state program.) In CBO's projection, combined Medicare and Medicaid spending increase from 5.3% in 2009 to as much as 10.0% in 2035 and 12.7% of GDP in 2050, at which point total health care spending is projected to exceed one-third of GDP. Medicare's dedicated revenues are also projected to stay relatively constant, so even under the most benign scenarios, these programs would put a serious strain on general revenues under current policy.[8] Even with the assumption that excess cost growth will slow, total health care spending (private and public) would be nearly half of GDP by the end of the projection window.

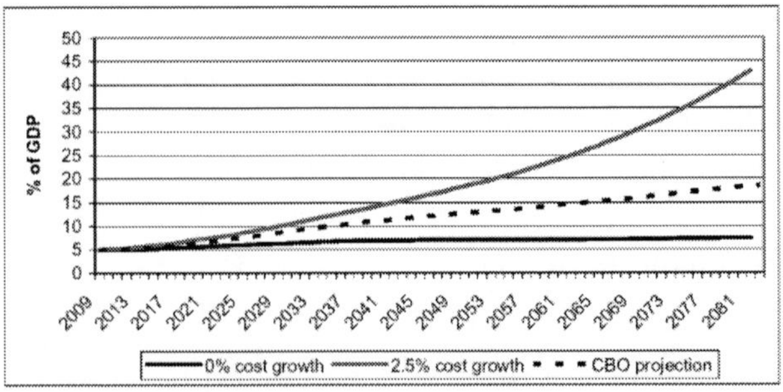

Source: Congressional Budget Office, *The Long-Term Budget Outlook*, June 2009.

Note: Excess cost growth refers to growth in spending per beneficiary above GDP per capita growth.

Figure 3. Projected Spending for Medicare and Medicaid as a % of GDP Under Various Assumptions about Excess Cost Growth

Although most of the policy debate in the past has focused on ways to reform Social Security, it is Medicare and Medicaid that place a far larger strain on the federal budget. Between now and 2035, Social Security spending is projected to increase by 1.2 percentage points, whereas Medicare and Medicaid spending is projected to increase by as much as 4.7 percentage points of GDP. From 2035 to 2050, Social Security spending as a share of GDP is projected to decrease by 0.3 percentage points, whereas Medicare and Medicaid spending is projected to increase by 2.7 percentage points.

Other government spending programs will also be affected by an aging society, including Supplemental Security Income (SSI) and health and pension spending for civil servants and veterans.[9] Some analysts fear that the finances of the Pension Benefit Guarantee Corporation, a government agency that insures private defined benefit pension plans, could also be negatively affected if firms do not take steps to improve their pension reserves.[10] (On the other hand, government spending on the young could fall as a share of GDP as our society ages, although much of that spending is done at the state level.) The increase in projected spending for these programs is small as a share of GDP compared with the increases in Social Security, Medicaid, and Medicare spending, however. In 2000, Social Security, Medicare, and Medicaid accounted for about 85% of total federal spending on the elderly.[11]

It is also unclear what assumptions should be made to project current tax policy. If current law were followed, the 2001 and 2003 tax cuts would expire and an estimated 70% of taxpayers would eventually be subject to the alternative minimum tax (AMT) due to inflation. A projection more consistent with current tax policy would arguably be to assume that the tax cuts do not expire and the AMT is indexed for inflation. This projection results in a modest increase in revenues relative to GDP because of "real bracket creep," meaning that as incomes rise, taxpayers on average shift into higher tax brackets.[12] Likewise, discretionary spending is set annually through the appropriations process, so many valid assumptions could be made about its future size. An assumption that nondefense discretionary spending will stay close to its recent share of GDP is consistent with recent history and seems reasonable for a long-term projection.

Under the above assumptions about current policy and future excess cost growth, the increase in entitlement spending would not be matched by increases in general revenues or decreases in other spending, and would need to be entirely deficit financed. As a result, after briefly dipping to 7.4% of GDP in 2020, projected budget deficits would top 14% of GDP by 2035 and the national debt would rise at a continually accelerating pace and rapidly surpass record levels relative to GDP. If the tax cuts and AMT patch were assumed to expire (as scheduled under current law) and non-entitlement spending were reduced to all-time lows relative to GDP, deficits would rise more slowly, but still exceed 10% of GDP after 2050.

Another way to measure the imbalance in future government finances is through the fiscal gap concept, which refers to the immediate reduction in spending or increase in taxes that would be required in order to prevent the federal debt from rising relative to GDP over the projection window.[13] CBO estimates a fiscal gap of 8.1% of GDP over the next 75 years under current policy. To close this fiscal gap today, would require immediately reducing total non-interest spending by 32%, raising total revenues by 52%, or some combination of the two. Although these changes would be unprecedented, delay would require even larger cuts in the future. Waiting until 2020 to change policy would increase the fiscal gap to 9.7% of GDP, and waiting until 2040 would increase it to 15.5% of GDP, necessitating more drastic adjustments. Although these options are undesirable, they cannot be postponed indefinitely (if the projections prove to be accurate) for reasons discussed in the next section. Policymakers do have a wide array of choices concerning the form the tax increases or spending cuts could take, however.

The Effects of Current Policy on the Economy

Figure 4 illustrates why current policy is considered to be unsustainable. Large budget deficits would cause the national debt to rise at an accelerating rate to unprecedented levels. If current policy is maintained, the deficit would decline to 7.4% in 2020, which would not be small enough to prevent the debt from continuing to grow relative to GDP. After 2020, the deficit would rise rapidly.

Before 2009, the United States had never financed a peacetime deficit above 6% of GDP and foreign countries have not succeeded in financing persistent deficits that were much larger. Although larger U.S. deficits were financed during wars, wars are only temporary, whereas the fiscal imbalance under current law is permanent. In essence, the rise in entitlement spending under a scenario with continued excess cost growth is too large and permanent to credibly be financed indefinitely by pushing its cost forward through borrowing.

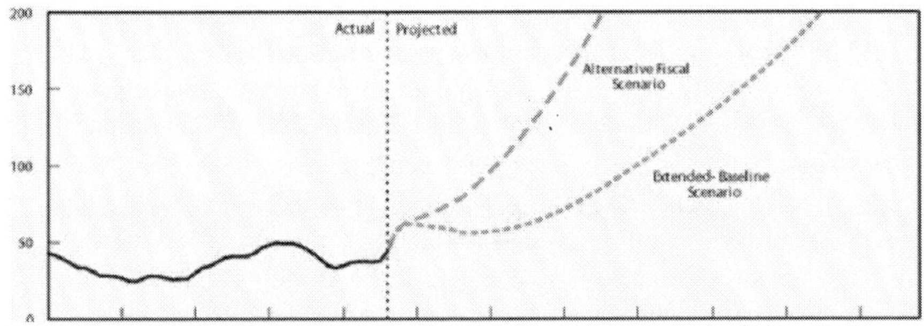

Source: Congressional Budget Office, *The Long-Term Budget Outlook*, June 2009.

Notes: The alternative fiscal scenario assumes that current policy is maintained. The extended-baseline scenario assumes that the tax cuts and AMT patch expire and discretionary spending grows at the rate of inflation for the next 10 years.

Figure 4. Projected Federal Debt as a Share of GDP

If current policy is maintained and the assumptions in the projections hold, the resulting deficits would likely cause interest rates on U.S. Treasury bonds to rise substantially, both as a result of the higher risk that the Treasury might ultimately default on its debt and also because the government's demand for borrowed funds would raise the price of credit, which is the rate of interest. Default would likely undermine financial stability because of the central role that U.S. Treasury securities play in providing the financial system with liquidity, as a benchmark asset, and as a "safe haven" for risk averse investors. If the government financed its rising budget deficit by increasing the money supply, the rate of inflation would also increase significantly along with interest rates. Budget deficits of the size projected under current law could lead investors to doubt that the United States would be able to service its debt fully and on time, which could cause the value of the dollar to drop precipitously. Because more than one-half of the total outstanding debt of the United States is held abroad, a collapse of the dollar would have serious economic repercussions around the world.

Presumably, U.S. budget policies will be altered before this point is reached. In the interim, the deficit would still have a negative impact on the economy long before the fiscal outlook reached crisis. A rising risk premium due to an unsustainable fiscal policy is only one reason for interest rates to rise. The deficit also causes interest rates to rise because it is competing with private capital investment to be financed from a finite pool of loanable funds from domestic and foreign lenders. Interest rates rise to equilibrate the higher demand for credit with the supply of loanable funds, which is national saving plus capital from abroad. The deficits projected under current policy would exceed private saving and cause national saving to become negative.

Whatever the cause of the increase in interest rates, the effect on the economy is the same: higher interest rates reduce private capital investment. Lower rates of capital formation cause economic growth to slow, leading to lower U.S. living standards (as measured by per capita income) in the long run than there otherwise would have been. Foreign capital flows can offset part or all of the decline in national saving, but this will still result in lower U.S. standards of living than if the budget had been balanced because the income from that capital will flow to foreigners instead of Americans.[14] CBO estimates that, by 2045, the deficits resulting from current policy would reduce the capital stock by more than 35% and gross national product by 16% relative to what it would have been.

Even if future budget deficits were reduced to the point where they became sustainable, crowding out still results in a smaller future economy than would otherwise be the case, all else equal. As a result, fewer resources would be available in the future from which the government can draw to finance the retirement of the baby boomers. Ultimately, the resources available in the economy as a whole will determine the level of government spending that is feasible in the future. Financing a given level of spending from an economy that is smaller than it would have been in the absence of deficits would, in turn, require higher tax rates.

CBO long-term budget projections do not include any of the macroeconomic effects discussed in this section—the projected deficits are not assumed to affect interest rates or GDP through crowding out effects. If macroeconomic effects were included, the projections would be more unfavorable—interest payments on the national debt would be higher and tax revenues would be lower.

Why Can't the Contributions of Young Workers Finance the Benefits That They Have Been Promised?

Proposals to eliminate the shortfall of revenues in the future to finance the entitlement benefits that have been promised under current law have raised criticisms about fairness. After all, retirees today paid the same or lower tax rates than today's workers, and they are receiving the benefits equal to (or exceeding) what they were promised. While this predicament may be perceived as unfair, it is inherent in a pay-as-you-go system where benefits are based on income and financed by those working at the time. When the worker-retiree ratio falls, only two options are available under pay-as-you-go: benefits to retirees fall or taxes on workers rise. A pay-as-you-go system is fundamentally different from the fully funded pension systems that private employers run, where an employee's contributions are invested to finance his future benefits, rather than used to pay the benefits of current retirees. (Even a fully funded pension system would pay smaller monthly annuities when life expectancy rose, however.)

Once a pay-as-you-go system is up and running and suffers an adverse demographic shift, there is no reform that can avoid placing a burden on some participants in the system by making some present or future generation receive less than past generations. This burden can be thought of in terms of generations participating in the system, rather than in terms of taxes and benefits. For example, the burden imposed by a tax on today's workers is equivalent to the burden of a benefit cut when today's workers retire. Reform cannot avoid making some current or future generations pay disproportionately because the windfalls initially created by a pay-as-you-go system have already been collected and spent by the early workers in the system who received benefits that far exceeded their contributions.[15]

Evaluating the generational equity of a reform proposal is best done from a government-wide perspective, and not from a programmatic perspective. For example, proposals can appear to raise entitlement benefits paid to any given generation through general revenue transfers or increasing the national debt. But general revenue transfers or a larger national debt must (eventually) be financed through higher taxes or lower government spending. Thus, the burden has been shifted out of the program and into the general budget—it has not been reduced.

Trust Funds Cannot Finance Future Benefits from a Government-Wide Perspective

According to law, when benefit costs of Social Security and Medicare Part A exceed income, their trust funds can be drawn down to finance benefits. It is often argued that benefits can be financed in full until their trust funds are exhausted, which is projected to occur in 2036 and 2016, respectively. (Medicare Part B does not have a dedicated revenue source and relies heavily on general revenue transfers already.)[16] While this is true from the programs' perspective, the trust fund "assets" have no effect on solvency from the overall government's perspective. The trust funds hold U.S. Treasury securities, which are nothing more than an IOU from the government to the trust fund. Therefore, Social Security and Medicare can only be financed in full as long as the government can find the budgetary resources to finance them. Arguing that the trust fund securities provide those resources is equivalent to arguing that one has assets because one's right pocket contains an IOU from one's left pocket. The problem is not that, from the trust fund's perspective, the government will not honor its Treasury securities. The problem is that, from the government's perspective, it must find the budgetary resources to honor those securities. Under current policy, it will lack the resources before the trust funds are exhausted because tax revenue is not projected to rise nor nonentitlement spending projected to fall in tandem with the rise in entitlement spending.

If the trust fund surpluses created future budgetary resources at the time they were accumulated, then those surpluses could be thought of as having a valid economic "claim" on those resources (although the political process would still determine whether they received their claim). Unfortunately, the government's overall fiscal position has precluded the possible use of the surpluses to create future budgetary resources. With the exception of 1999-2000, surpluses of the Social Security and Medicare systems have not been—and are still not being—used to improve the government's fiscal condition in preparation for the retirement of the baby boomers. Instead, they are being used to support the government's current fiscal stance, in which revenues and other outlays are set at a level where they are not in balance. If the surpluses were being saved, they could be given "credit" for freeing up future budgetary resources, and an argument could be made that those freed-up resources should then be devoted to the entitlement programs. But since they are being diverted to finance nonentitlement spending, the presence of trust fund surpluses has not created any future budgetary resources that can be used by future governments to honor the Treasury securities held by the trust funds. It is the government's unwillingness to balance revenues and outlays outside the trust funds that prevents the trust fund surpluses from generating real resources that can be drawn down in the future.[17]

Focusing the reform debate on the government's overall fiscal position rather than the position of the program's trust fund also would have the benefit of avoiding budgetary maneuvers that may give the false appearance that the programs' fiscal position has been improved. For example, some reform proposals return the trust funds to solvency through general revenue transfers or by "investing" the entitlement surpluses in nongovernmental financial assets (either collectively or through individual accounts) without increasing the government's tax revenue. Although these proposals make the programs' financial position look improved in isolation, they do nothing to reduce the overall imbalance between government outlays and government revenues. In the case of the latter, surpluses diverted from financing general government outlays for "investment" purposes must be replaced by increasing the national debt in the absence of other policy changes.

For the government as a whole, higher earnings on the trust funds or individual accounts are offset by higher interest on the national debt.

ECONOMICEFFECTS OF REFORM OPTIONS

Reform may encompass several goals—altering the redistributive characteristics of the system, giving people more choices about the form their benefits take, and so on. This section considers reform options in light of only one goal—altering current policy to achieve future fiscal solvency—because changes to the status quo are unavoidable under current projections. Achieving this goal is possible only through some combination of higher tax revenues and lower spending;[18] as demonstrated above, maintaining current policy through borrowing is unsustainable. In CBO's projection, Medicare and Medicaid spending grow continually relative to GDP. While clearly unrealistic as a "best guess" of future outcomes, it may make sense as a projection of current policy, for it underlines the fact that any policy changes to place the budget on a sustainable path must include reductions in the growth rate of government health spending.

Although the fiscal problems facing the government in the future are large, they are also distant. Budgetary resources are available for policy to continue along its current course for at least another decade or two. In this light, before evaluating specific reform proposals, it is useful to explore the arguments for not postponing reform further. Reforming now rather than later has been justified on at least three grounds: to reduce the scope of future policy changes, to improve inter-generational equity, and to reduce uncertainty.

Prefunding to Reduce the Scope of Policy Changes

One reason given to undertake reform today is to reduce the scope of the policy changes that must be ultimately undertaken. Reform, as defined in this chapter, reduces the government's overall future fiscal shortfall. Reforms made today can reduce the future fiscal shortfall without reducing the present fiscal shortfall. For example, a benefit cut could be announced today that did not go into effect until, say, 2030. But for reform to reduce the ultimate scope of future benefit cuts or tax increases, it must incorporate *prefunding—raising resources today and saving them so that more resources are available in the future to pay future benefits*. In other words, a smaller benefit cut could restore fiscal solvency if it went into effect today and its proceeds were saved than if it went into effect in 2030. For example, CBO estimates a fiscal gap (the immediate tax increases or spending cuts needed to stabilize the federal debt) of 8.1% of GDP over the next 75 years under current policy. Waiting until 2020 to change policy would increase the fiscal gap to 9.7% of GDP, and waiting until 2040 would increase it to 15.5% of GDP.

Prefunding can be done through the government (by paying down the national debt or investing the trust funds in private assets) or through individual accounts. The salutary effects of prefunding on the projected future fiscal imbalance are not limited to changes in Social Security and Medicare. Any policy change that reduced the current budget deficit would reduce the government's future fiscal gap; likewise, current budget deficits increase that fiscal gap. Prefunding increases the resources available to the government and economy as a whole by raising the national saving rate.[19] The additional saving is then available to finance additional capital investment spending (or reduce reliance on foreign saving to finance current investment), which increases national output. A greater national output increases the future resources available to finance the needs of an aging population, and reduces the government's fiscal shortfall.[20] The current fiscal stance of budget deficits, by contrast, eliminates the prefunding that would presently occur if the Social Security surpluses were saved and exacerbates the future fiscal shortfall for the same reasons. But making the transition to a prefunded system makes current generations worse off, because the prefunding must be financed either through higher taxes or lower benefits.

Prefunding requires higher revenues since under pay-as-you-go, existing revenues are already financing the benefits of current beneficiaries. (And because of the on-budget deficit, trust fund surpluses are already financing other government spending.) If reform were instead financed through borrowing, it would not improve the government's ability to pay benefits in the future (after adjusting for risk)—it would saddle future generations with explicit general government liabilities, in the form of a greater national debt. If reform is financed by borrowing, the increase in national saving in the trust fund or individual accounts is offset one for one by the decrease in government saving through the larger budget deficit.

Because benefits are tied to wages and GDP, prefunding not only increases the resources available to finance existing benefits promised by current law, it also increases the benefits themselves. (Prefunding leads to some fiscal improvement because it does not increase the Social Security benefits of those already retired.) To make prefunding a more effective strategy for improving future fiscal solvency, benefits could be de-linked from economic growth. De-linking Social Security benefits from economic growth is straightforward and can be accomplished by no longer tying benefits growth to wage growth. De-linking Medicare benefits from economic growth is less straightforward—as long as demand for health care increases with income, policies to increase GDP are also likely to increase the demand for Medicare spending.

Plans to reform through prefunding face a difficult political dilemma: how can a commitment to prefund be maintained and reform plans preserve a course of action that spans decades in the face of the comings and goings of new Congresses every two years? If reform plans cannot be preserved, little may be gained, from an economic perspective, by reforming now.[21] This is a particular concern since there could potentially be significant short-term political gains and few political costs from diverting prefunding resources to unrelated policy goals. History suggests that this concern is a real one: for example, the congressional "Social Security lock box" failed to prevent Social Security surpluses from being diverted to finance other spending beginning in 2001.[22] For this reason, prefunded individual accounts might have an important political advantage over centralized government prefunding because they take those resources "off the table" politically so that they could not be diverted to other uses. However, it is important to note that if individual accounts are debt-financed rather than prefunded, they will not be taking any resources "off the table."[23] Proponents argue that a centrally controlled trust fund invested in private assets would be another way to take those resources "off the table." Opponents argue that the earnings of a centrally controlled trust fund could be siphoned off to finance other government spending just as easily as the interest earnings of the trust funds are siphoned off today.

Inter-generational Equity

Another reason given for undertaking reform sooner rather than later is to pursue intergenerational equity. The choice for policymakers is whether to spread the tax increases or spending cuts over all generations beginning now through prefunding, or whether to concentrate the policy changes on future generations. Financing government spending through budget deficits does not impose less of a burden than tax increases or other spending cuts—it shifts the burden forward to future generations through a lower saving rate and capital stock.[24] The longer reform is postponed, the greater the benefit reductions or tax increases imposed on future generations. Economic theory cannot judge the desirability of a reform that shifted to prefunding because it is a question of inter-generational equity: is it "fair" that future generations are treated worse than current and past generations under current policy because of the effects of adverse demography on a pay-as-you-go system? Prefunding would place less of a burden on future generations, but would be unlikely to eliminate it since past generations received benefits that exceeded their contributions. Under current policy, the Trustees report for Social Security and Medicare estimated, respectively, that there will be a transfer of resources from future generations to past and present generations of workers equal to $16.3 trillion for Social Security and $14.2 trillion for Medicare in present value terms.[25] Some would argue that it is fairest to spread the unavoidable burdens of a pay-as-you-go system among all generations, rather than placing the entire burden on future generations. Others would argue that placing the burden on future generations is justified since they will be wealthier than current generations because of future economic growth. In the case of Medicare and Medicaid, another argument against current generations bearing more of the burden is the uncertainty about whether projected spending increases will actually materialize.

Deciding between benefit reductions and tax increases to restore future fiscal solvency is often viewed through the prism of fairness. This is somewhat misleading—in the aggregate, there is not much difference in fairness between cutting benefits and raising taxes on the same individual. For equity considerations, the generation affected by the reform is more important than the form that reform takes. Reforms undertaken now can raise taxes or lower benefits on current generations or future generations; reforms postponed to the future will only affect future generations. However, Social Security does provide favorable benefits to individuals who are low-income, widows, dependents, and the disabled, and maintaining the favorable treatment they currently receive would depend on the nature of the benefit cuts.

Reducing Uncertainty

Finally, another rationale for undertaking reform sooner rather than later is that it can reduce uncertainty. Workers trying to plan their optimum private saving behavior today are hampered by uncertainty concerning the benefits that will be provided by the government in the future. Some policy uncertainty is caused by the projected future fiscal shortfall, and can be reduced if the shortfall is reduced. On the other hand, there is forecast uncertainty, which complicates attempts to modify policy ahead of time, since policy responses could turn out to be larger or smaller than what turns out to have been needed. As demonstrated in Figure 3, the correct rate of future excess cost growth for Medicare and Medicaid is the largest source of long-term forecast uncertainty.

Uncertainty has implications for the types of reforms that can be undertaken. Policy options that affect individuals when they are old must be adopted far ahead of time if individuals are to be given time to adapt to those changes. For example, benefit cuts must be announced far in advance if individuals are to be given the opportunity to save more in their working years to offset benefit cuts. By contrast, policy options that affect individuals when they are young, such as tax increases, can be adopted more rapidly. This implies that postponing reform is likely to bias the eventual resolution toward tax increases rather than spending cuts.

Reform Options: Reducing Benefits

Social Security[26]

Relatively minor changes in benefit calculations could bring Social Security outlays back in line with revenues under the intermediate scenario.[27] For example, if initial benefits were indexed to price inflation instead of wage growth, outlays would fall significantly in the long run. If this were done, benefits would still be rising in nominal terms (and keeping constant in real terms), but the replacement rate of benefits compared to wages would fall. The advantage of this approach would be that savings to the government would rise over time (as the spread between wages and prices grew) to offset the increasing fiscal imbalance. (Since budgetary savings grow under this approach, larger reductions would be needed if postponed to the future.) A disadvantage of this proposal is that it is not directly tied to the size of the financial shortfall, so if the shortfall turned out to be smaller (larger) than expected, benefits would be cut more (less) than needed to restore solvency. CBO estimated that one proposal along these lines could reduce outlays under current policy to 4.1% of GDP from 5.8% of GDP by 2050.[28] This would keep Social Security spending near its current level as a share of GDP.

To avoid a reduction in their standard of living in retirement following a benefit cut, workers may choose to save more of their income during their working years or work longer. Thus, to the extent that Social Security substitutes for private saving, benefit cuts could lead to higher saving or labor supply which, in turn, would boost economic growth.[29] But to the extent that Social Security substitutes for family income transfers, households fail to plan ahead for retirement saving, or private saving is driven by other motives, such as a bequest motive or precautionary saving, reduced Social Security benefits would not influence private saving. Furthermore, the relatively unequal distribution of U.S. wealth suggests that private saving may not be that sensitive to changes in Social Security. At the top of the income distribution, which accounts for most U.S. saving, Social Security makes up little if any of an individual's retirement income. For example, elderly in the highest quartile of the income distribution received 20% of their income from Social Security in 2008.[30] At the bottom of the income distribution, a sizable fraction of Americans have very little private saving, and would presumably suffer a reduction in living standards rather than raise their saving rate in light of a benefit cut.[31]

An alternative approach to reducing benefits would be to raise the retirement and early retirement ages. This approach could avoid reducing monthly benefit payments, although lifetime benefits would fall since retirees would begin to collect benefits later in life. Proponents justify this approach on the grounds that rising life expectancy means that retirees are collecting benefits for longer than previous retirees—in effect, longer life expectancy has inadvertently caused lifetime benefits to increase. In addition, raising the retirement age would directly increase output by keeping workers in the labor force longer, thereby providing the economy as a whole with more resources to cope with an aging society. One study estimates that raising the retirement age to 70 would increase employment rates among men age 55-74 by as much as 15%, or total employment among men by 3%.[32] CBO estimated that a proposal to raise the retirement age and adjust early retirement benefits would reduce outlays in 2050 from a projected 5.8% of GDP under current policy to 5.0% of GDP.[33]

Medicare and Medicaid

Unlike Social Security, there are no straightforward proposals to reduce the long-term growth in Medicare and Medicaid spending. Social Security spending is based on specific formulas that can be altered to reach a desired spending level. Health spending, by contrast, is not currently set directly by the government. Rather, the government chooses the services it will finance, and the spending on those treatments ultimately depends on supply and demand. Little is known about how much long-term savings could be garnered from some of the proposals discussed below; it is likely that none of the proposals adopted in isolation could close the entire fiscal imbalance.[34] Restraining long-term health cost growth has been considered extensively in the 111th Congress's debate on health care reform, but to date CBO has concluded that the proposals would have a small effect on health spending relative to future budget deficits, and the budgetary savings generated would be at least partly offset by other parts of comprehensive reform bills that would tend to increase health spending.[35]

The central challenge for policymakers is to reduce excess cost growth. If spending on the health programs grew at the rate of GDP, they would not place a significant strain on government finances. However, there is no way to know what rate of excess cost growth will occur in the future. Forecasters assume that the rise in health spending will outpace GDP growth because it has consistently done so in the past. It is possible that technology or consumer preferences would change on their own such that excess cost growth wanes without government intervention. But it may be more prudent to assume that it will not wane, given historical patterns. Then the challenge becomes finding policy actions that can restrain excess cost growth.[36] Some economists argue that there are structural biases toward excess cost growth in the market for health care that could be altered by policymakers.

Policymakers can attempt to restrain cost growth through the demand side or supply side of the market. Demand could be reduced by shifting Medicare costs from the government to the beneficiaries, which would also directly reduce the government's fiscal gap and alter generational equity, if applied to current generations. (Shifting costs to the beneficiaries in the Medicaid program is arguably less philosophically compatible since it is a low-income support program.) Demand could be reduced by making beneficiaries bear a greater portion of Part B premiums.[37] (If desired, higher premiums could be means-tested to avoid negative effects on low-income individuals.) Beneficiaries currently pay about 25% of premiums and general revenues pay the remainder. However, higher premiums may have little effect on medical spending of participants (although it could reduce participation) since it would not influence the marginal cost of specific treatments (because premiums finance the overall insurance, not specific treatments). To influence marginal costs, raising deductibles and co-insurance rates would be more effective. But even if marginal costs were increased, some analysts are skeptical that consumers could make well-educated decisions based on price since choosing between medical procedures, unlike most goods, involves a highly specialized knowledge of medicine. And unless rules on supplemental coverage were altered, privately-purchased supplemental plans or Medicaid could cancel out policy changes that made marginal costs higher and shift health spending from Medicare to private spending and Medicaid.[38]

Another way to reduce demand would be to restrict enrollment. One way would be to raise the age of eligibility. In fact, unlike Social Security, Medicare's eligibility age is not already rising under current law. Modifying Medicare's eligibility age to match Social Security's would save billions of dollars, but the saving would still be modest in light of the program's future projected fiscal shortfall.[39]

Budgetary savings is not a rationale for reducing demand in and of itself. From an economic perspective, reducing demand is desirable if the benefits of receiving the health care are outweighed by the costs to society of their provision. Medicare may provide a service (elder health care) that could not be as efficiently provided by the market, notably because of adverse selection.[40] If higher costs to beneficiaries caused them to drop out of Part B or receive too little care (notably preventive care), Medicare spending could fall to a socially sub-optimal level. (Non-participation could be avoided by making participation mandatory, although this would increase budgetary pressures). On the other hand, since patients do not directly bear the costs, medical care may be over-consumed at present from a society-wide perspective, which would make a reduction in demand more economically efficient.

On the supply side of the market, spending could be reduced by restricting the medical services that the government will reimburse or limiting the coverage of newly developed treatments. Consequences of such an approach are that some medical spending would cease and some would be shifted to private spending and private insurance.

Some argue that another path to restraining cost growth lies with transforming Medicare from a government monopsony to a competitive market of private insurers, including the health maintenance organization (HMO) model that dominates employer-based coverage.[41] (This approach is sometimes referred to as "premium support.") The rationale behind this argument is that government lacks the profit-incentive, competitive pressures, and market savvy needed to restrain costs.

Others argue that government provision has two advantages over competition that make it more suitable. First, only government has monopsony bargaining power and economies of scale (which it does not fully use at present), and these can be used to hold down costs more effectively.[42] Second, an efficient insurance mechanism broadly pools risk so that the premiums of the healthy offset the costs of the sick. Health insurance could only be efficiently provided in competitive markets if adverse selection and cherry picking (private plans only serving healthy individuals to lower costs) could be avoided. Theoretically, adverse selection could be avoided through some combination of nondiscriminatory coverage, risk-adjusted premiums, and Medicare regulating the types of coverage that any plan must provide, but designing these tools effectively has been difficult in practice.[43] In any case, as an empirical matter, HMOs do not have a long enough track record to reach a consensus on whether they can reduce costs continually or only on a one-time basis. Although many analysts credit HMOs with reducing cost growth following their adoption in the 1990s, cost growth accelerated again in this decade.[44]

For the HMO model to reduce Medicare spending, it would have to be set up differently than the current Medicare Advantage system.[45] In the Medicare Advantage system, the government sets the minimum beneficiary premiums, the basic benefits offered, and the payments to companies. Thus, companies are not really free to compete on price, and efficiency gains cannot be translated into lower spending. Instead, companies compete on the medical services offered (they must offer a basket of services set by the government and can add additional services to that basket), so that, holding government-mandated premiums constant, efficiency gains are translated into higher profits or greater medical spending (because the company will offer the beneficiary more medical services). Preventing companies from competing on price is a way to reduce (but not likely eliminate) adverse selection; for companies to compete on price and the market to function efficiently, other tools would need to be found to prevent adverse selection.

Some analysts argue that reforms to Medicare's payment system could also generate cost savings. Health care providers are paid on a fee-for-service basis, which may give them an incentive to over-provide. Medicare payments are set by complex formulas that may not always match the price that Medicare could secure if bargained in the market. Once a treatment is approved by Medicare, the government leaves it to physicians, who have little incentive to consider the government's objective of limiting spending, to prescribe its use. Some researchers argue for "evidence-based medicine," claiming that cost-saving could be achieved by substituting less expensive treatments that are similarly effective.[46] For example, some researchers claim that the differences in outlays by region cannot be explained by cost of living and patient characteristics.[47] However, these types of reforms may lead to one-time, rather than continuous, cost savings.

Two other proposals to limit supply meet skepticism among economists. First, queuing (rationing under-supply through waiting lists) is widely used to reduce costs in foreign countries with nationalized health care systems. But economists are skeptical that the benefits of the lower financial costs exceed the nonfinancial costs of queuing. The nonfinancial cost can be thought of as the monetary price patients would be willing to pay to avoid the wait. Second, cutting Medicare's payments to providers cannot be used to restrain cost growth on an ongoing basis. While this strategy has been used in the past for short-term budgetary savings, to use it on an ongoing basis would require providers to accept continually lower payments for their services. Eventually, this would cause providers to withdraw their services, and some analysts have argued that this has occurred when payments have been cut in the past.

When evaluating all of the proposals made above, consider whether the goal of reform is to reduce federal spending or economy-wide spending on elderly health care. Answering this question is beyond the scope of this chapter, but many economists doubt that excess cost growth could be reduced in Medicare and Medicaid unless it is also reduced in private health care spending.[48] In other words, private corporations, insurers, and medical providers would have to change their behavior in order for health spending (and the budget) to be placed on a sustainable path. Some of these changes in private spending may come about through private sector initiatives and some through public policy changes. Many proposals could potentially replace Medicare spending with private spending, either by individuals or by the corporations from which they retired, or spending by state and local governments. Some proposals, adopted in isolation, would shift some spending from Medicare to Medicaid, which would limit the proposal's budgetary saving. Since Medicaid is a jointly funded state-federal program, there is frequently tension to shift costs back and forth between the two when either is looking to reduce overall spending.

Reform Options: Raising Taxes

The projected tax increases required to place Social Security back on a solvent financial path are not large compared with historical changes in tax revenues. If Social Security is maintained on a pay-as-you-go basis, tax increases of 1.2% of GDP are projected to be needed by 2050 (assuming, because of the overall budget shortfall, that general revenues are unavailable).[49] To place this total in perspective, tax revenues increased by 2.5 percentage points of GDP between 1993 and 1999, with little evidence of negative ramifications for the economy. If taxes are increased sooner and the revenues saved, the projected increase required to bring the system back to solvency is smaller.

Projected tax increases required to keep Medicare and Medicaid on sustainable paths and maintain benefits are much more daunting. Net spending on Medicare and Medicaid is projected to rise 7.8 percentage points of GDP by 2050. Gradual tax increases of these magnitudes need not be ruled out as infeasible since many Western European countries collect more than 50% of GDP in tax revenue, compared with 29% of GDP for the total of state, local, and federal government in the United States in 2007. Alternatively, if there were no excess cost growth, taxes would need to increase by 2 percentage points of GDP by 2050.

If reform relied on tax increases, what form could they take? Social Security and Medicare Part A are currently financed largely through payroll taxes, but could be financed in any way in the future (with or without a dedicated revenue source).

If taxes were levied on individuals, they could take the form of wage (payroll) taxes, income taxes, or consumption taxes. (If levied on corporations, other options would be available.) Tax revenue can also be raised at existing tax rates by broadening the tax base, an approach often favored by economists. Consumption and wage taxes affect labor supply but not saving decisions; income taxes affect both. Income taxes have a broader base and require lower tax rates in the long run. Wage or income tax increases could be made more progressive through a graduated rate structure; progressivity would be harder to achieve with consumption taxes. Consumption taxes would shift more of the burden of reform to the existing elderly because they tax existing saving when it is drawn down.

Besides tax rate increases, there could be changes made to the tax treatment of Social Security to raise revenue. For example, if policymakers wanted to make the system more progressive, the income ceiling on the payroll tax could be removed for Social Security (there is none for Medicare). Alternatively, Social Security benefits could be taxed in full (currently about two-thirds of recipients pay no tax on their benefits). (Whether these changes are consistent with the overall tax system depends if Social Security is viewed as a pension or income transfer system.) Revenues could be raised within Medicare through higher premiums for Parts B or D.

If the long-term fiscal imbalance were closed through higher taxes, raising taxes earlier and saving the proceeds through prefunding would require smaller tax increases than if tax increases were postponed. Earlier tax increases would be more economically efficient than larger increases later, and would affect generational equity by shifting some of the cost of reform to present generations. If taxes were raised today and the proceeds not saved, then the tax increases required in the future would not be reduced.

There is a widespread belief that lower spending is better for economic growth than higher taxes, but there is not strong evidence backing this belief. Economic theory is ambiguous as to the effects of higher taxes on growth in general, and it would also depend on what form the tax increase took. Either way, empirical evidence suggests that the economic effect is small for modest changes. In the case of closing the fiscal gap, however, the estimated changes are much larger. CBO estimates that eliminating the overall fiscal shortfall through higher marginal taxes would cause the economy to be 5% to 20% smaller in 2050 compared to if government spending were cut (under this projection, the economy would still be much larger than it is today).[50] CBO notes that there is little confidence surrounding these estimates since there is no comparable historical experience and little consensus over what model best describes how taxes affect the economy. Furthermore, CBO notes that the economic effects would be significantly smaller if revenue were raised by broadening the tax base instead of by raising marginal rates.

Taxes can affect economic growth by influencing labor supply (both the decision to work and the number of hours worked) or the saving rate. Empirical evidence is inconclusive as to the effects of taxes on saving because the decision to save is a very complicated one made over time and motivated by many different factors. Thus, results turn out to be highly sensitive to the model used. Currently, Social Security and Medicare Part A are financed by payroll taxes, which do not affect saving. However, even under the assumption that tax increases had no effect on the decision to save at the margin, raising taxes by several percentage points of GDP could reduce private saving by reducing after-tax income. Empirical evidence suggests that labor supply is relatively unresponsive to tax changes—most people, particularly men and single women, will work full-time regardless of tax rates.[51] In any case, individuals would not be expected to change their behavior as much in response to an increase in taxes for Social Security compared with a normal tax increase, because reducing labor supply would directly reduce the individual's benefits.

One demographic group whose labor supply may be more sensitive to tax rates is the elderly and near-elderly. This suggests that reform options that affect the (implicit or explicit) tax rate on the elderly could have important effects on the economy, even when those policies are intended to reduce entitlement spending. When entitlement spending is influenced by current income, spending policies can also act as a tax by reducing benefits when income rises.[52]

Some argue for reform based on tax increases on the grounds that recent tax cuts have contributed to the overall future shortfall between projected revenues and outlays. For example, the recent tax cuts, EGTRRA (P.L. 107-16 and JGTRRA (P.L. 108-27), have been estimated to increase the "fiscal gap," the long-term budget deficit, by 2.2% of GDP. To offset the effects of these tax cuts on the fiscal gap, an estimated 9% permanent reduction in all (noninterest) spending would be required.[53]

Reform Options: Individual Accounts

Individual accounts have been proposed as a potential solution to Social Security's financing problems.[54] Proponents argue that payroll tax revenues could be diverted to accounts that would be owned by the individual, and these accounts could be invested in financial securities. The high rate of return earned by the accounts, it is argued, could be used to reduce Social Security's fiscal shortfall.

Switching Social Security to a system of individual accounts, partially or completely, raises several economic issues that will not be addressed in this chapter, including questions of risk sharing, adverse selection, moral hazard, annuitization, and bequests.[55] Furthermore, individual accounts alone would not address the system's current social goals, which include redistribution and the provision of benefits for survivors, dependents, and the disabled, which currently accounted for approximately 37.6% of the system's outlays in 2008.[56]This chapter will only analyze the claim that individual accounts can improve the government's fiscal position.

As illustrated below, individual accounts would not be self-financing because savings to the government from the individual accounts would not occur until the account holders retire. All payroll tax revenues are currently dedicated to the payment of benefits to current retirees or the financing of general government spending—despite the Social Security surplus, there are no unused funds available to finance the creation of individual accounts. Thus, individual accounts would need to be financed by immediately raising taxes, reducing spending, or issuing Treasury securities (increasing the budget deficit); this is sometimes referred to as the "transition cost" of implementing individual accounts.[57]

Individual accounts are one vehicle through which prefunding can be implemented if financed through higher taxes or lower government spending. Then, all else equal, the government's overall fiscal position will improve, national saving will rise, private investment will increase, and this will increase the future size of the economy.[58] As noted above, individual accounts are not necessary for prefunding—prefunding can also occur if the government reduces the national debt or collectively invests in private securities. However, individual accounts may also be created without prefunding by increasing the size of the budget deficit.[59] If this occurs, no additional economic resources will be generated to reduce the government's fiscal imbalance. Any gain in government revenues from the individual accounts will in theory be offset by higher interest payments on the national debt (because the individual accounts were debt financed) and a lower rate of return earned by private investors (because the increased demand for private securities and government debt would push down the return on private securities and raise the interest rate that the government must pay to finance its debt). If individual accounts equal to 2%-4% of payroll (0.8%-1.6% of GDP) were introduced without a new source of revenue, as President Bush's Commission to Strengthen Social Security proposed in August 2001, the effect on interest rates and private rates of return could be significant. The creation of debt-financed individual accounts is a zero sum game for the economy as a whole because they do not raise the national saving rate (the rise in private saving is canceled by the decline in public saving) nor the national capital stock, all else equal, so they do not increase national income. Most proposals do not allow accounts to be "topped up" with voluntary private contributions, so there is little reason to think that the increase in private saving will exceed the decrease in private saving.[60]

This argument can be made more concrete using official estimates provided by Social Security Administration actuaries of Option 1 in President Bush's Commission to Strengthen Social Security. In Option 1, workers under

55 could elect to deposit 2% of their OASDI taxable earnings in an individual account, with an offsetting reduction in benefits based on diverted amounts compounded at a real rate of return 3.5%, which is the source of budgetary saving to the government. Since Option 1 does not identify any new source of revenue to finance the accounts, they can be considered to be debt-financed. It is analyzed here because it is the only option that relies solely on individual accounts (Options 2 and 3 are a combination of individual accounts and benefit reductions.)

Figure 5 illustrates the *change* in the income and cost rates of the Social Security system as a percentage of taxable payroll caused by introducing individual accounts.[61] Diverting 2% of the payroll tax to individual accounts would reduce the income rate by an amount that would stabilize at about 1.33% of taxable payroll in a decade, assuming two-thirds of eligible workers participate. However, individual accounts would not lead to any significant decline in the cost rate for many years, since funds would not be withdrawn from individual accounts (which reduces the cost rate through the Social Security benefit offset) until they retire. The reduction in the cost rate steadily increases over time, approaching 2.75% of payroll in 2075, as larger individual accounts are amassed and then drawn down. For the first 40 years after the introduction of individual accounts, the accounts are projected to generate less revenue than was being diverted from beneficiaries. Roughly 40 years after the introduction of individual accounts, when enough retirees had spent their entire career making contributions, the reduction in benefits from the offset would exceed the revenue lost from a 2% marginal payroll tax cut. After that, the savings to the government would grow and eventually become large.[62]

Thus, individual accounts would exacerbate the financing problems of the Social Security system for roughly 40 years, but improve the system's finances from that point on. Whether this is desirable can only be determined by judging the effect of the accounts on the economy and government as a whole. Such accounts would improve the government's overall finances and national saving only if the revenue shortfalls caused by them in the first 40 years of their existence were financed through tax increases or benefit reductions.[63] By contrast, Figure 6 illustrates the projected *increase* in the unified budget deficit compared with current policy if the individual accounts are debt financed (i.e., introduced without an accompanying source of financing).[64] As explained above, the effect on the unified budget balance is the most meaningful measure because it is the only one that clearly identifies the cost of reform to the government as a whole.

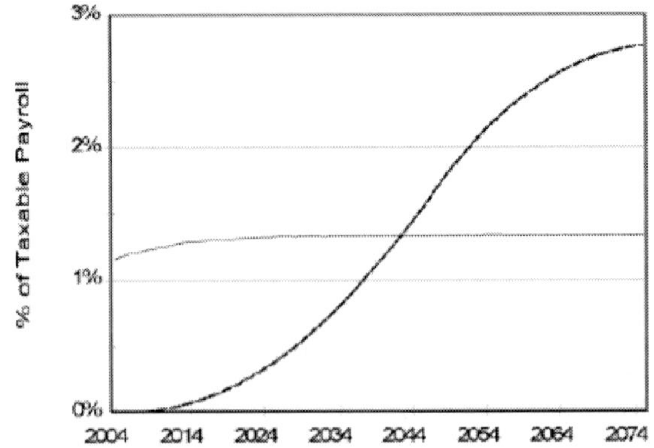

Source: Chief Actuaries of Social Security Administration, *Memorandum to President's Commission to Strengthen Social Security*, December 2001, p. 53.

Notes: Estimates based on Commission's Option 1 reform plan with 66.7% participation rate. It assumes accounts equal to 2% of payroll are introduced in 2004.

Figure 5. Change in Social Security's Finances From Introducing 2% Individual Accounts

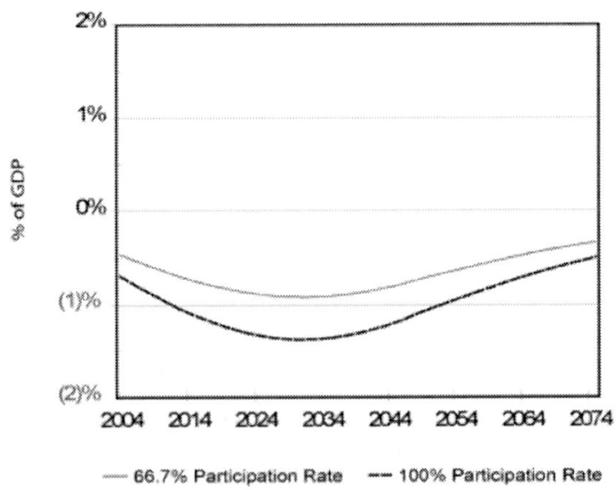

Source: Chief Actuaries of Social Security Administration, *Memorandum to President's Commission to Strengthen Social Security*, December 2001, pp. 53-54.

Note: Estimates based on Commission's Option 1 reform plan with 66.7% and 100% participation rate. It assumes accounts equal to 2% of payroll are introduced in 2004. Negative number signifies an increase in the deficit.

Figure 6. Change in Unified Budget Balance From Introducing 2% Debt-Financed Individual Accounts

Over the first 40 years of the accounts' existence, the decline in the income rate would exceed the decline in the cost rate, and the government would have to borrow the difference, increasing the national debt and interest payments on the debt. Once the decline in the cost rate exceeded the decline in the income rate, the effect of the individual accounts on the budget would be positive; however, this saving would be offset by the higher interest payments on the larger national debt. As long as the additional interest payments on the debt plus the decline in the income rate exceed the decline in the cost rate, the net effect of the individual accounts on the budget deficit would be negative. Figure 6 indicates that individual accounts, if debt financed, *worsen the government's fiscal shortfall through 2075.*[65]

Because the private assets in individual accounts are growing through the accumulation of interest, these results may seem puzzling. Although the assets in individual accounts are growing, the debt issued by the government to finance the accounts is also growing because of interest accumulation. The individual accounts offset government benefits at a higher rate of return than the interest payments on government debt (3.0%), so eventually (outside the 75-year window) the individual accounts save the government money. (It is the benefit offset, not the earnings of the accounts, that reduce the government's liabilities.) But because so much debt must be issued immediately, it takes more than 75 years before the accounts pay for themselves. In fact, the actuaries of the SSA make two sets of assumptions, both of which are illustrated in Figure 6. Since the accounts are voluntary, they estimated the costs under the assumptions (1) that 66.7% of eligible individuals elect to participate, and (2) that 100% elect to participate. Comparing the results under the two assumptions leads to a result that may buck conventional wisdom: when individual accounts are debt financed, the cost to the government can be reduced by reducing the participation rate.

President Bush's Commission on Social Security made it clear that Option 1 would not avert a future financing crisis.[66] For that reason, it also proposed two further options that coupled the introduction of individual accounts with benefit reductions. But it follows from the data presented on Option 1, that it is only the benefit reductions, not the individual accounts (if debt financed) that improve the system's financial position in Options 2 and 3 through 2075.

Depending on the details, some individual account proposals could worsen the government's fiscal outlook by adding benefits or administrative costs to the current Social Security system. Many proposals allow the individual account's balance to be left as a bequest to heirs when the owner dies; when an individual (and, if applicable, his widow or her widower) dies prematurely in

Social Security, the excess of taxes paid over benefits collected improves the system's financing. Individual accounts may require regulatory oversight financed from general revenues (e.g., to ensure that the accounts are not being invested fraudulently.) The government may feel obligated to "bail out" individual accounts with general revenue in the event of a stock market crash. Individual accounts may receive better or worse tax treatment than Social Security benefits, which would worsen or improve the government's finances, respectively. For example, 100% of withdrawals from traditional individual retirement accounts (IRAs) are taxed, while 0% to 85% of Social Security benefits are taxed (depending on income level). However, contributions to IRAs are deducted from taxable income, while the employee's half of Social Security contributions (payroll taxes) are not. If withdrawals from individual accounts receive the same tax treatment as IRAs, it would increase tax revenues; if contributions receive the tax treatment of IRAs, it would decrease revenues.

It should briefly be noted that the economic benefit of introducing individual accounts is unrelated to its effects on government finances. The economic benefit of individual accounts is that it could potentially lead workers to view Social Security less as a tax and benefit program and more as a pension. If so, it could reduce the distortions to work and save currently caused by Social Security. For example, workers may be more likely to continue working after they become eligible for retirement if they can continue accumulating contributions in their individual account, whereas the increase in Social Security benefits from working after normal retirement age are relatively small.[67] Whether these distortions are sizable, or even necessarily reduce growth, is an open question among economists. These economic benefits of switching to individual accounts would need to be weighed against the economic costs, which include problems of moral hazard, adverse selection, and less risk pooling.[68] If features are added to the accounts to reduce the economic costs, the economic benefits will also tend to be reduced.

CONCLUSION

The budget deficit reached 10% of GDP in 2009, an unsustainable level in the long run in the sense that it would cause the federal debt to continually grow faster than national income. While entitlement spending on the elderly had little to do with the recent increase in the deficit, it is the main reason why the deficit is projected to remain at high and rising levels in the long run under current policy. The retirement of the baby boomers, increased life expectancy, and the rising cost of health care are projected to make current policy unsustainable in the long run. Increases in spending are not expected to subside after the baby boomers have passed away. To keep the overall budget on a sustainable path over the next 50 years, either the projected rise in Social Security, Medicare, and Medicaid spending will have to be contained, or tax revenues will have to be increased, or both. Determining the right balance between benefit reductions or tax increases depends on people's desire to spend future income gains on health vs. non-health consumption expenditures, and whether those expenditures can be more efficiently and fairly supplied by the private sector or government programs. (Based on CBO projections, reduction in the growth of Medicare and Medicaid has to be part of the solution since it continually outpaces GDP growth.)

If current policy is maintained until 2030, CBO projects that some combination of tax increases and spending reductions totaling 12.1% of GDP would be needed at that point to place the budget on a sustainable path for the next 75 years. However, if reforms are made ahead of time, the ultimate size of required tax increases or benefit reductions could potentially be reduced. For example, CBO projects that immediate action would reduce the needed tax increases or benefit reductions to 8.1% of GDP. For this to occur, the revenues generated through tax increases or benefit cuts would have to be dedicated to a higher rate of public saving, thereby boosting economic growth. If the revenues are instead spent on other government spending or tax cuts, the ultimate size of future benefit cuts and tax increases will not have been reduced. Grappling with the fiscal solvency issue is also complicated by the inability to bind future Congresses to a long-term spending path—even if revenues raised are initially used to reduce the budget deficit, there is the risk that the fiscal improvement will be undone by future Congresses.

Determining how much benefits and revenues should be altered ahead of time is difficult, however, because of the wide degree of uncertainty associated with long-term government projections. In particular, if the projected future excess medical cost growth does not materialize, the budget outlook would dramatically improve. Crafting a solution to restore fiscal solvency faces the fundamental question of how much can be done at this point to prevent excess cost growth that has not yet happened—and may never happen. On the other hand, acting in advance may expand the array of feasible options. Restoring the system to solvency ahead of time would allow individuals enough forewarning that they could adjust to future benefit reductions without disrupting their spending patterns—for this reason, if reform is postponed, it is more likely to result in tax increases since notions of fairness make benefit cuts to those already retired unlikely.

What has already contributed to the fiscal imbalance is today's budget deficits, and the simplest and most concrete step that can be taken to reduce the fiscal gap is to reduce the current budget deficit. The salutary effects of prefunding on the future fiscal imbalance are not limited to changes in Social Security and Medicare. Any policy change that reduced the current budget deficit would reduce the government's future fiscal gap; likewise, current budget deficits increase that fiscal gap. The budget deficit in 2009 exceeded total net spending on Social Security, Medicare, and Medicaid—thus, placing the budget on a sustainable path in the near term cannot be accomplished solely through a focus on entitlement spending.

Social Security faces a financial imbalance that experts agree can be eliminated through relatively small increases in taxes and decreases in benefits,[69] and the changes could be minimized if they were prefunded today. The system faces no immediate financial shortfall—on the contrary, it is currently generating surpluses, so it is the only part of the budget that is not contributing to current budget deficits. It would not put pressure on the rest of the budget in its current state until at least 2016, according to the Social Security trustees. Individual accounts are not a substitute for benefit cuts or tax increases, although they could be a vehicle for either. Debt-financed individual accounts, by themselves, are projected to worsen the fiscal outlook over the next 75 years and not increase GDP through higher national saving.

Medicare and Medicaid face much larger and more intractable financial problems than Social Security. Historically, health care spending generally, and health care spending on the elderly in particular, have risen much more rapidly than has overall economic output. It is impossible to know if this pattern will continue in the future, but if it does, Medicare and Medicaid under current policy risk overwhelming budgetary resources. Yet unlike Social Security, spending on the health programs cannot be controlled directly unless access is restricted or rationed. To reduce future Medicare and Medicaid spending, the government must find a way to reduce the price or quantity of elderly health care provided. Quantity can be reduced either through restrictions on the medical treatments offered or by lowering demand. Demand could possibly be reduced through higher costs to the recipient, but the link between price and demand will always be indirect in an insurance program since marginal costs are largely borne by the insurer (in this case, largely the government), rather than the insured. Continually reducing prices on the supply side cannot be accomplished simply by continually reducing payments to providers. Ultimately, if payments decline and providers' costs do not, providers may stop offering those services. For that reason, many experts doubt that a reduction in Medicare and Medicaid cost growth can be sustained without a reduction in private health care cost growth. On the supply side, technological improvements or efficiency gains could in theory reduce future prices, although in recent years they have led to higher prices by making new (but expensive) treatments available. It is unclear what interventions government can pursue to reverse that trend. Certain modifications have been suggested that might lead to one-time efficiency gains, such as changes to the Medicare reimbursement system or the adoption of private sector HMO administration. But it is less clear that these modifications could lead to the continuous efficiency gains required to contain cost growth.

End Notes

[1] All projections in this chapter come from Congressional Budget Office, *The Long-Term Budget Outlook*, June 2009, unless otherwise noted. Similar projections can be found in Government Accountability Office, *The Nation's Long-Term Fiscal Outlook*, GAO-09-405SP, April 30, 2009; Office of Management and Budget, *Budget of the U.S. Government, Analytical Perspectives, Fiscal Year 2010*, May 2009, Ch. 13.

[2] Entitlement spending has risen over the past decade as the overall budget has shifted from surplus to deficit, but this rise in spending was anticipated and would not have been large enough to cause a budget deficit absent other policy changes. It was primarily those other policy changes, as well as a deterioration in economic conditions in the past year, that caused the budget to be in deficit when it had previously been projected to remain in surplus. For more information, see CRS Report R40435, *Budget Deficits: An Explanation of How Policy Affects Budget Balance*, by Mindy R. Levit and Marc Labonte.

[3] An exception is the portion of Medicare Part B which is financed through premiums paid by the elderly. About one quarter of Part B spending is paid through premiums and the other three quarters is paid by taxpayers, and can be considered to be financed on a pay-as-you-go basis. Part of Medicare Part D, the prescription drug benefit, will also be paid for by the elderly through premiums when implemented. A small fraction of Social Security's revenues also comes from the taxation of some Social Security benefits. Disability benefits are also part of the Social Security system.

[4] Data from Congressional Budget Office, *Long-Term Projections for Social Security: 2009 Update*, August 2009.

[5] Medicaid covers much long-term care spending and health spending for the lower-income elderly. CBO estimates that approximately 22% of all Medicaid spending is on the elderly.

[6] Glen Follette and Louise Sheiner, "The Sustainability of Health Spending Growth," Federal Reserve Board of Governors, *Finance and Economics Discussion Series 2005-60*, September 2005.

[7] The 2.5% excess cost growth assumption is included for illustrative purposes; as noted above, it is not possible for spending to rise that quickly over the projection window.

[8] Estimates of Medicaid spending presented here are for federal Medicaid spending only; state governments are also projected to see a large increase in future Medicaid spending. Estimates of Medicare spending are net of premiums paid by recipients.

[9] For more information, see CRS Report 94-486, *Supplemental Security Income (SSI): A Fact Sheet*, by Scott Szymendera.

[10] Sylvester Schieber and John Shoven, "The Consequences of Population Aging for Private Pension Fund Saving and Asset Markets," *The Economic Effects of Aging in the United States and Japan* (Chicago: University of Chicago Press, 1997), p. 111.

[11] Congressional Budget Office, *Federal Spending on the Elderly and Children*, July 2000.

[12] Withdrawals from tax-deferred saving vehicles have been projected to lead to only a small increase in revenues when the baby boomers retire, and may be more than offset by other factors that make revenues fall. Alan Auerbach, William Gale, and Peter Orszag, "Reassessing the Fiscal Gap: The Role of Tax-Deferred Saving," *Tax Notes*, July 28, 2003.

[13] Although some modest increase in the debt relative to GDP is sustainable, it is uncertain how much. Therefore, the fiscal gap assumption is a commonly used rule of thumb for estimating sustainability.

[14]See CRS Report RL31775, *Do Budget Deficits Push Up Interest Rates and Is This the Relevant Question?*, by Marc Labonte.

[15] See Henning Bohn, "Social Security Reform and Financial Markets," in Steven Sass and Robert Triest, eds., *Social Security Reform*, Federal Reserve Bank of Boston, Conference Series 41, June 1997, p. 196; John Geanakopolis, Olivia Mitchell, and Stephen Zeldes, "Social Security Money's Worth," NBER Working Paper 6722, September 1998.

[16] Congressional Budget Office, *Long-Term Projections for Social Security: 2009 Update*, August 2009; and The Board of Trustees of the Federal Hospital Insurance and Federal Supplementary Medical Insurance Trust Funds, *2009 Annual Report*, May 12, 2009.

[17] Some argue that the surpluses have created real resources because the government's unified budget deficit would have been even larger had it not been for the trust fund surpluses. This argument cannot be settled conclusively since there is no way of knowing the size of the unified budget deficit in the counterfactual case where there had not been Social Security surpluses. For a comparison of perspectives on the trust fund, see Kent Smetters, "Is The Social Security Trust Fund Worth Anything?," *National Bureau of Economic Research*, Working Paper 9845, July 2003.

[18] For an overview of Social Security reform and current legislation, see CRS Report RL33544, *Social Security Reform: Current Issues and Legislation*, by Dawn Nuschler.

[19] It should be noted that from an economic perspective, increasing resources available to the government is not important, since theoretically the government can raise taxes to any level they desire at any time. It is the increase in the resources of the economy that is important.

[20]See CRS Report RL30708, *Social Security, Saving, and the Economy*, by Brian W. Cashell

[21] Bosworth and Burtless present international evidence that saving in a public pension system is offset by dissaving in the rest of the government's budget. Barry Bosworth and Gary Burtless, "Pension Reform and Saving," working paper presented at the International Forum of Collaboration Projects, Tokyo, Japan, February 17-19, 2003.

[22] See CRS Report RS20165, *Social Security and Medicare "Lock Boxes"*, by David S. Koitz and Geoffrey C. Kollmann.

[23] Peter Diamond argues that these resources would not really be "off the table" because there would be political pressure to allow pre-retirement withdrawals from the accounts, as is allowed for individual retirement accounts (IRAs), and to substitute withdrawals from the accounts for government spending. See Peter Diamond, "Macroeconomic Aspects of Social Security Reform, *Brookings Papers on Economic Activity 2*, 1997, p. 1.

[24]See CRS Report RL30520, *The National Debt: Who Bears Its Burden?*, by Marc Labonte.

[25] The transfers could be considered underestimates because they do not include the $2.7 trillion combined trust fund assets that have been used to finance other government spending or the general revenue transfers to finance Parts B and D of Medicare equal to $18.7 trillion that

financed the benefits of past and present generations. Some of these general revenues will be paid by future generations and some by present generations. See Tables III.C16 and III.C24 of the Medicare Trustees' Report and Table IV.B7 of the Social Security Trustees' Report.

[26] Proposed benefit reductions to close the fiscal gap are relative, not absolute, reductions. If future generations receive only the benefits that can be financed by dedicated revenues under current law, their dollar amount will still exceed the benefits paid to retirees today. However, these benefits will be lower relative to earnings because future earnings and life expectancy will be higher. (Likewise, tax increases would reduce after-tax income as a share of future income, but would still leave future citizens with higher incomes than today in absolute terms.) Similarly, under current law, even though the retirement age has increased, future retirees will spend more years in retirement collecting benefits than current retirees because of increases in life expectancy.

[27] The effect of a number of reform proposals on system solvency can be found in Social Security Advisory Board, *Why Action Should Be Taken Soon*, (Washington, DC: July 2001). The report also illustrates how much larger reforms would need to be if postponed.

[28] Congressional Budget Office, *Budget Options*, August 2009, p. 143.

[29] See Barry Bosworth and Gary Burtless, "Supply Side Consequences of Social Security Reform: Impacts on Saving and Employment," Center for Retirement Research at Boston College, Working Paper 2004-1, January 2004.

[30] CRS Report RL32697, *Income and Poverty Among Older Americans in 2008*, by Patrick Purcell.

[31] See James Poterba, "Discussion," in Steven Sass and Robert Triest, eds., *Social Security Reform*, Federal Reserve Bank of Boston, Conference Series 41, June 1997, p. 146. Data can be found in CRS Report RL32697, *Income and Poverty Among Older Americans in 2008*, by Patrick Purcell.

[32] See Barry Bosworth and Gary Burtless, "Supply Side Consequences of Social Security Reform: Impacts on Saving and Employment," Center for Retirement Research at Boston College, Working Paper 2004-1, January 2004, p. 38.

[33] Congressional Budget Office, *Budget Options*, August 2009, p. 145.

[34] Ten-year cost estimates for many Medicare reform proposals can be found in Congressional Budget Office, *Budget Options, Volume 1: Health Care*, December 2008.

[35] See, for example, Congressional Budget Office, *Patient Protection and Affordable Care Act, Incorporating the Manager's Amendment*, December 19, 2009. See also Congressional Budget Office, *Health Care Reform and the Budget*, June 16, 2009.

[36] There are conceptual difficulties with the idea that a policy change today can prevent excess cost growth from occurring over the next 75 years, when it is impossible to know whether it would have happened anyway. In this case, it would not be known if attempts to solve the problem had worked until well after the fact.

[37] Revenue estimates for raising premiums and other reform options can be found in Marilyn Moon, Misha Segal, and Randall Weiss, "A Moving Target: Financing Medicare for the Future," *Inquiry*, vol. 37, no. 4, Winter 2000/2001, p. 338. For example, the authors find that roughly quadrupling premiums in 2025 would raise government revenues by about 2% of GDP.

[38] See Government Accountability Office, *Medigap*, GAO-02-533T, March 14, 2002.

[39] See, for example, Congressional Budget Office, *Cost Estimate of S. 947/H.R. 2015 as passed by the Senate on June 25, 1997*, July 2, 1997. Because of changes to Medicare since this cost estimate was conducted, it should be viewed as giving only an order of magnitude estimate to the cost savings of the proposal.

[40] Adverse selection is caused by asymmetric information because patients know more about their health conditions (and therefore, potential medical costs) than insurers. Because of asymmetric information, sick patients will find an average price offered by insurers

profitable and healthy patients will find it unfavorable. As a result, healthy patients could be driven out of the market, driving average prices up.

[41] Jonathan Oberlander, "Is Premium Support the Right Medicine for Medicare?," *Health Affairs*, vol. 19, no. 5, September/October 2000, p. 86.

[42] Health spending as a share of GDP has stabilized in the past few years in many advanced economies with government run single-payer health care systems. It is not clear that the policies responsible for this experience can be translated for the decentralized health sector of the United States. See Organization of Economic Cooperation and Development, *Health Data 2009*, July 1, 2009.

[43] As an example of how adverse selection may already affect Medicare, some analysts argue that HMOs providing Medicare+Choice plans are only profitable because they attract enrollees more healthy than the average but are paid by Medicare according to the average. See Barbara Cooper and Bruce Vladeck, "Bringing Competitive Pricing to Medicare," *Health Affairs*, vol. 19, no. 5, September/October 2000, p. 55.

[44] For example, see Marsha Gold, "Can Managed Care and Competition Control Medicare Costs?," *Health Affairs*, Web Exclusive, April 2, 2003.

[45] For more information, see CRS Report RL32618, *Medicare Advantage Payments*, by Paulette C. Morgan and HindaChaikind.

[46] For studies of variations in medical treatments and outcomes, see Dartmouth Atlas of Health Care, "Dartmouth Studies Show Wide Variation in Hospital Care and Outcomes For Chronically Ill Medicare Patients," press release, October 7, 2004.

[47] Uwe Reinhardt, "Health Care for the Aging Baby Boom: Lessons from Abroad," *Journal of Economic Perspectives*, vol. 14, no. 2, Spring 2000, p. 71.

[48] See, for example, Organization for Economic Cooperation and Development, *Economic Survey: United States*, vol. 2007/9, May 2007, ch. 3.

[49] Trustees of OASDI, *Annual Report, 2009*, Table VI.F4.

[50] Congressional Budget Office, "The Long-Term Economic Effects of Some Alternative Budget Policies," *Letter to the Honorable Paul Ryan*, May 19, 2008.

[51] See Theresa Devine, "Demographics, Social Security Reform, and Labor Supply" and Eric Engen and William Gale, "Effects of Social Security Reform on Private and National Saving," both in Steven Sass and Robert Triest, eds., *Social Security Reform*, Federal Reserve Bank of Boston Conference Series 41, June 1997, p. 77; Congressional Budget Office, *Labor Supply and Taxes*, memorandum, January 1996; Jerry Hausman, "Taxes and Labor Supply," Alan J. Auerbach and Martin Feldstein, eds., *Handbook of Public Economics*, vol. 1, New York, North Holland, 1985; CRS Report RL31949, *Issues in Dynamic Revenue Estimating*, by Jane G. Gravelle.

[52] For example, after a worker has accumulated 35 years of Social Security contributions, additional payroll taxes may exceed the further increases in benefits that they produce. Features of Social Security, Medicare, and tax policy like these cause the overall implicit "tax on work" after the age of 62 to far exceed the actual tax rate. One study shows that for a representative worker, the implicit marginal tax on work rises from 14.2% at age 55 to 24.7% at age 62 to 39.4% at age 65 to 49.5% at age 70. In other words, at age 70 a worker can only increase his after-tax and after-benefit spending by 50 cents for every dollar earned. These calculations are based on a representative worker who is a single male with a defined contribution pension. Women and married men with working spouses face somewhat lower implicit marginal tax rates. Barbara Butrica et al., "Does Work Pay at Older Ages?," Center for Retirement Research at Boston College, Working Paper 2004-31, November 2004.

[53] Alan Auerbach, William Gale, and Peter Orszag, "Sources of the Long-Term Fiscal Gap," *Tax Notes*, May 24, 2004, p. 1049.

[54] Similar proposals have been made by some for Medicare but have not received any congressional attention. See Martin Feldstein, "Prefunding Medicare," *National Bureau of Economic Research*, Working Paper 6917, January 1999. In his proposal, individual

accounts would accumulate savings that could then be used to purchase health insurance upon retirement. See also Thomas Saving, "Making the Transition to Prepaid Medicare," *Journal of Economic Perspectives*, vol. 14, no. 2, Spring 2000, p. 85; and Laurence Seidman, "Prefunding Medicare Without Individual Accounts," *Health Affairs*, vol. 19, no. 5, September/October 2000, p. 72.

[55] These issued are comprehensively analyzed in CRS Report RL31498, *Social Security Reform: Economic Issues*, by Jane G. Gravelle and Marc Labonte.

[56] Trustees of OASDI, *Annual Report, 2009*, Table III.A5.

[57] See CRS Report RS22010, *Social Security: "Transition Costs"*, by Laura Haltzel.

[58] This assumes that the individual accounts are "carved out" of the existing Social Security system through benefit offsets and diverting some of the payroll tax. Some policymakers have instead recommended that the accounts be "added on" to Social Security by not altering present law benefits and not diverting the payroll tax. The effects of "add on" accounts on the economy are the same as "carve outs": if the accounts are financed through higher taxes or lower spending, then they will increase national saving (although less than one for one because there will be some offset in private saving), which will increase GDP. But if they are financed through larger budget deficits, they will not contribute to national saving, and therefore not increase GDP. However, no matter how they are financed, "add on" accounts do not reduce the government's fiscal gap because they do not reduce Social Security's liabilities nor introduce a new revenue stream that can be used to finance Social Security's liabilities.

[59] According to media reports, the Bush Administration stated that this was its plan at an economic summit in December 2004. Edmund Andrews, "Bush Puts Social Security at Top of Economic Conference," *New York Times*, December 15, 2004.

[60] Since the individual accounts do not reduce the government's fiscal gap, individuals with "rational expectations" would not be expected to respond to the creation of the accounts by reducing their private saving. Nevertheless, if individuals perceived the individual accounts as new net wealth to them, they might decide that they need to save less to meet their retirement needs.

[61] The income rate refers to payroll tax revenue collected by the Social Security system. The cost rate refers to the benefits paid by the Social Security system. Taxable payroll is the tax base from which payroll revenues are collected.

[62] Since the graph shows the *change* in the income and cost rates caused by introducing individual accounts, a future financing crisis is averted only if the proposals generate enough additional revenues to cover the entire financing gap.

[63] The accounts are unlikely to raise private saving by more than the fall in public saving, since the accounts come from tax revenue and cannot be supplemented by private saving contributions.

[64] This graph does not illustrate the overall budget deficit under a system of individual accounts, but rather the *change* in the budget deficit caused by the introduction of individual accounts.

[65] At some point beyond the 75-year projection window, the effect of introducing debt-financed individual accounts on the budget deficit may turn positive, but projections of a long enough duration to answer that question are not available.

[66] President's Commission to Strengthen Social Security, *Final Report*, December 2001, p. 15.

[67] Barry Bosworth and Gary Burtless, "Supply Side Consequences of Social Security Reform: Impacts on Saving and Employment," Center for Retirement Research at Boston College, Working Paper 2004-1, January 2004.

[68] The economic costs and benefits of the current system compared with a system of individual accounts are analyzed in CRS Report RL31498, *Social Security Reform: Economic Issues*, by Jane G. Gravelle and Marc Labonte.

[69] For examples of specific proposals, see Peter Diamond and Peter Orszag, *Saving Social Security* (Washington, DC: Brookings Institution Press, 2004).

In: Federal Budget Outlook and Economic... ISBN: 978-1-61761-769-0
Editors: Michael S. Okada

Chapter 3

THE FEDERAL GOVERNMENT'S LONG-TERM FISCAL OUTLOOK

United States Government Accountability Office

GAO'S LONG-TERM FISCAL SIMULATIONS

Since 1992, GAO has published long-term fiscal simulations of what might happen to federal deficits and debt levels under varying policy assumptions. We developed our long-term model in response to a bipartisan request from Members of Congress who were concerned about the long-term effects of fiscal policy. More recently, GAO has also begun publishing separate long-term fiscal simulations for the state and local government sector. Additional information on both simulations is available at http://www.gao.gov/special.pubs/longterm/index.html.

GAO runs two simulations:

- "Baseline Extended" follows the Congressional Budget Office's (CBO) January 2010 baseline estimates for the first 10 years and then simply holds revenue and spending other than large entitlement programs constant as a share of gross domestic product (GDP).
- The "Alternative" simulation is based on historical trends and policy preferences. Discretionary spending grows with GDP rather than inflation during the first 10 years, Medicare physician payment rates

are not reduced as in CBO's baseline, all tax provisions are extended to 2020, and the alternative minimum tax (AMT) exemption amount is indexed to inflation through 2020; revenues are then brought back to their historical level.

This update incorporates CBO's most recent baseline projections that were released in January 2010.

The economic downturn and the federal government's response continue to shape the near-term budget outlook. In fiscal year 2009 the overall federal deficit reached 9.9 percent of GDP—the largest since 1945, and the deficit is expected to decline only slightly in 2010. While deficits are projected to decrease further as federal support for states and the financial sector wind down and the economy recovers, the increased debt and related interest costs will remain. Our long-term simulations show that absent policy changes the federal government faces an unsustainable growth in debt. Under our Alternative simulation, debt held by the public as a share of GDP could exceed the historical high reached in the aftermath of World War II by 2020 (see figure 1)—10 years sooner than our simulation showed just 2 years ago.

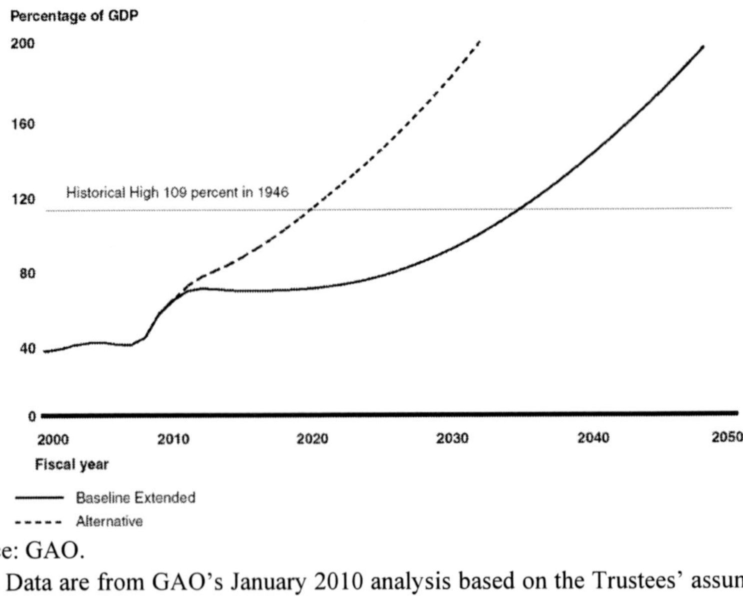

Source: GAO.

Note: Data are from GAO's January 2010 analysis based on the Trustees' assumptions for Social Security and Medicare.

Figure 1. Debt Held by the Public under Two Fiscal Policy Simulations

Recent events have made the fiscal challenge greater. Although the economy is still fragile, there is wide agreement on the need to begin to change the long-term fiscal path as soon as possible without slowing the recovery because the magnitude of the changes needed grows with time. Congress recently enacted a return to statutory PAYGO and, in February, the President established a commission to identify policies to change the fiscal path and stabilize the debt-to-GDP ratio.

HEALTH CARE COSTS AND DEMOGRAPHIC TRENDS ARE ALREADYAFFECTING THE NEAR-TERM BUDGET OUTLOOK

While the drivers of the long-term fiscal outlook have not changed, the sense of urgency has. As the table below shows, many of the long-term challenges highlighted in past updates, including health care cost growth and the aging population, have already begun to affect the federal budget—in some cases sooner than previously estimated—and the pressures only grow in the coming decade. For example, Social Security cash surpluses have served to reduce the unified budget deficit. However, CBO recently estimated that due to current economic conditions the program will run small temporary cash deficits for the next 4 years and then, similar to the Trustees estimates, run persistent cash deficits beginning in 2016. The fluctuation and eventual disappearance of the Social Security cash surplus will put additional pressure on the rest of the budget.

No one can say with certainty what the next 75-years will bring, but simulations by GAO, the Office of Management and Budget, CBO and others, which use some different assumptions, all show an unsustainable long-term fiscal path. For example, in the figure below, we compare the long-term outlook using two different sources for long-term Social Security, Medicare, and Medicaid projections (see figure 2). One of the key differences between these sources is the amount by which they assume the growth in health care costs per person exceeds the growth in GDP per person—what is known as "excess cost growth." Between 1975 and 2007, excess cost growth averaged 2.3 percent for Medicare and 1.9 percent for Medicaid. In the first set of simulations based on the Trustees' projections, excess cost growth averages 1.0 percent over the long term for both Medicare and Medicaid. In the second set based on CBO's projections, excess cost growth averages 1.5 percent over the long-term for Medicare and 0.6 percent for Medicaid. While the simulations using CBO assumptions yield less favorable outcomes, the results of these simulations are not materially different.[1]

Table 1. Challenges Affecting the Federal Budget in the Near Term

2008	Oldest members of the baby-boom generation became eligible for early Social Security retirement benefits
2008	Medicare Hospital Insurance (HI) outlays exceeded cash income
2010	Social Security runs first cash deficit since 1984[a]
2011	Oldest members of the baby-boom generation become eligible for Medicare
2014	45 percent of Medicare outlays funded by general revenue[b]
2016	Social Security begins running consistent annual cash deficits and redeeming trust fund assets (i.e., nonmarketable Treasury securities) in order to pay beneficiaries
2017	Medicare HI trust fund exhausted. Income sufficient to pay about 81 percent of benefits[b]
2020	Debt held by the public under GAO's Alternative simulation exceeds the historical high reached in the aftermath of World War II

Source: GAO.

[a] Based on CBO's January 2010 baseline projections.

[b] Based on *2009 Annual Report of the Boards of Trustees of the Federal Hospital Insurance and Federal Supplementary Medical Insurance Trust Funds* (May 12, 2009). Projections showing the percentage of funding from general revenue reaching 45 percent by law trigger a "Medicare funding warning," requiring a proposal from the President in response.

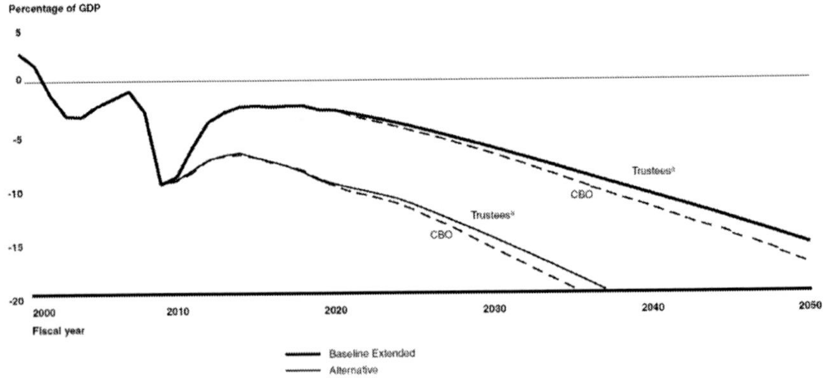

Source: GAO.

Notes: Data are from GAO's January 2010 analysis.

[a]Some adjustments are made to Trustees' assumptions.

Figure 2. Federal Surpluses and Deficits under Two Fiscal Policy Simulations with Different Entitlement Projections

Figures 3 and 4 show the composition of federal spending using different revenue and spending assumptions. In the Baseline Extended, discretionary spending is lower as a share of the economy and revenues are higher than the 40-year historical average. In the Alternative, both discretionary spending and revenue as a share of the economy are nearly at the historical averages. Both simulations show that absent changes to federal entitlement programs, spending on Social Security, Medicare, Medicaid, and interest on the federal debt will account for an ever-growing share of the economy. As figure 3 shows, assuming revenue remains constant at 20.2 percent of GDP—higher than the historical average—by 2030 there will be little room for "all other spending," which consists of what many think of as "government," including national defense, homeland security, investment in highways and mass transit and alternative energy sources, plus smaller entitlement programs such as Supplemental Security Income, Temporary Assistance for Needy Families, and farm price supports.

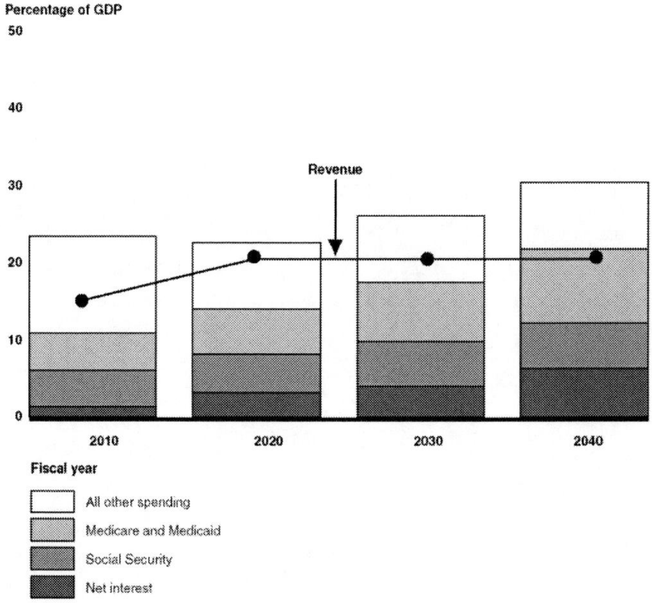

Source: GAO.

Note: Data are from GAO's January 2010 analysis based on the Trustees' assumptions for Social Security and Medicare.

Figure 3. Potential Fiscal Outcomes under the Baseline Extended Simulation: Revenues and Composition of Spending

In our Alternative simulation, which assumes expiring tax provisions are extended through 2020 and then revenue is held constant at the 40-year historical average, roughly 93 cents of every dollar of federal revenue will be spent on the major entitlement programs and net interest costs by 2020. By 2030, net interest payments on the federal government's accumulating federal debt exceed 8 percent of GDP—making it the largest single expenditure in the federal budget.

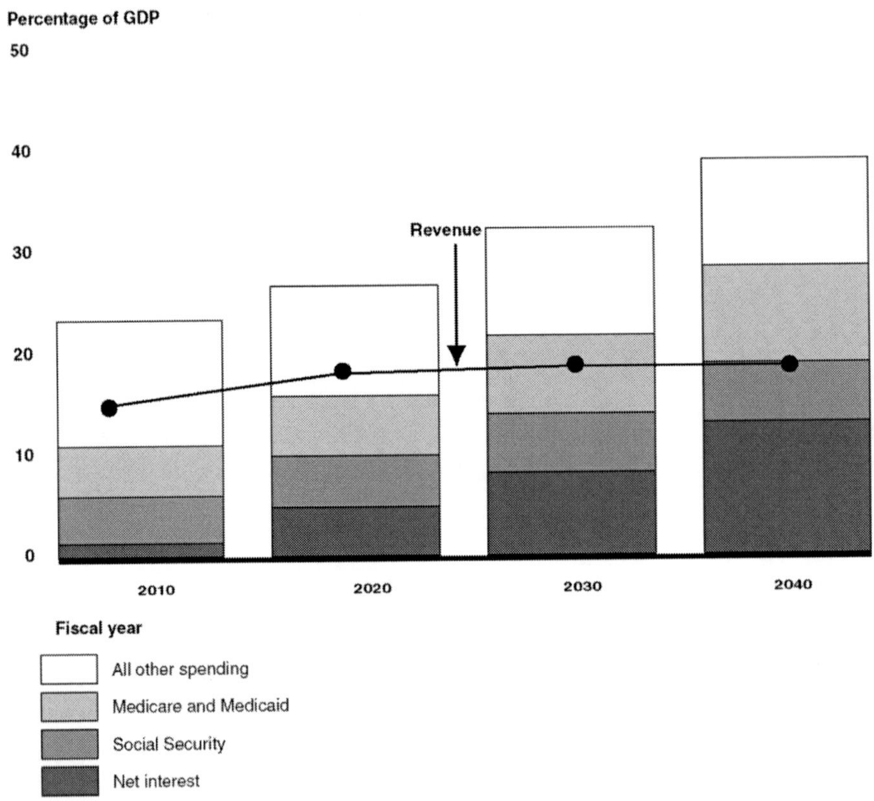

Source: GAO.

Note: Data are from GAO's January 2010 analysis based on the Trustees' assumptions for Social Security and Medicare.

Figure 4. Potential Fiscal Outcomes under the Alternative Simulation: Revenues and Composition of Spending

THE LONGER ACTION IS DELAYED, THE LARGER THE CHANGES NECESSARY

There are many ways to describe the federal government's long-term fiscal challenge. One method for capturing the challenge in a single number is to measure the "fiscal gap." The fiscal gap represents the difference, or gap, between revenue and spending in present value terms over a certain period, such as 75 years, that would need to be closed in order to achieve a specified debt level (e.g., today's debt to GDP ratio) at the end of the period.[2] From the fiscal gap, one can calculate the size of action needed—in terms of tax increases, spending reductions, or, more likely, some combination of the two—to close the gap; that is, for debt as a share of GDP to equal today's ratio at the end of the period. For example, under our Alternative simulation, the fiscal gap is 9.0 percent of GDP (or a little over $76 trillion in present value dollars) (see table 2). This means that revenue would have to increase by about 50 percent or noninterest spending would have to be reduced by 34 percent on average over the next 75 years (or some combination of the two) to keep debt at the end of the period from exceeding its level at the beginning of 2010 (53 percent of GDP).

Policymakers could phase in the policy changes so that the tax increases or spending cuts, or both, would grow over time allowing time for the economy to fully recover and for people to adjust to the changes.

Table 2. Federal Fiscal Gap under GAO's Simulations Based on the Trustees' Assumptions, 2010–2084

			Average percent change required to close gap			
	Fiscal gap		If action is taken today		If action is delayed until 2020	
	Trillions of present value 2009 dollars	Percent of GDP	Solely through increases in revenue	Solely through decreases in noninterest spending	Solely through increases in revenue	Solely through decreases in noninterest spending
Baseline Extended	41.1	4.8	24.2	20.0	29.1	23.4
Alternative	76.4	9.0	50.5	34.2	60.7	40.2

Source: GAO.

Note: Data are from GAO's January 2010 analysis based on the Trustees' assumptions for Social Security and Medicare.

However, the longer action to deal with the nation's long-term fiscal outlook is delayed, the greater the risk that the eventual changes will be disruptive and destabilizing. Under our Alternative simulation, waiting even 10 years would increase the fiscal gap to 11.0 percent of GDP—meaning a revenue increase of about 61 percent or a noninterest spending cut of about 40 percent or some combination of the two would be required to bring debt back to today's level by 2084.

STATE AND LOCAL GOVERNMENTS FACE SIMILAR FISCAL CHALLENGES

Rising health care costs are not only a federal problem; they are a national problem. GAO's most recent long-term state and local government simulations show that growth in health-related spending—Medicaid and health insurance for state and local employees and retirees—continues to be the primary driver of the long-term outlook at the state and local level. As we, CBO, and others have previously reported, the continued rise in health care costs also poses challenges to American businesses, families, and societies as a whole. Figure 5 overlays the simulated fiscal imbalance of the state and local government sector onto the Baseline Extended and the Alternative federal deficits. The overlay shows that the state and local governments' fiscal situation imposes further challenges for the nation's economy in the next several decades.

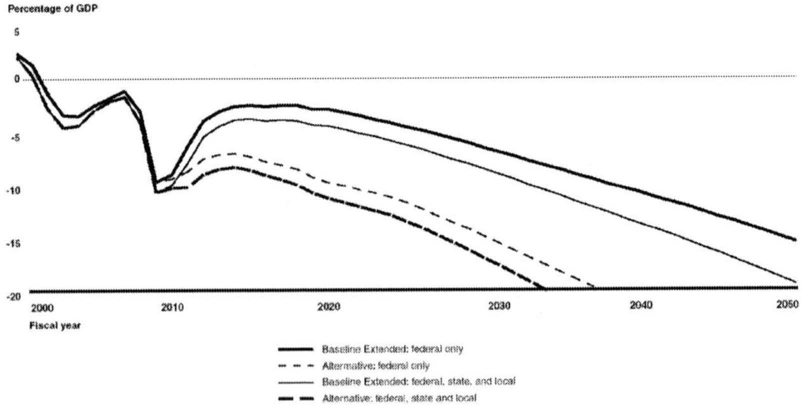

Source: GAO.

Figure 5. Federal and Combined Federal, State, and Local Surpluses and Deficits

RECENTDEVELOPMENTS

Our long-term simulations show that absent policy actions the federal government faces unsustainable growth in debt. Although the economy is still fragile, there is wide agreement on the need to begin to shift the long-term fiscal path as soon as possible without slowing the recovery. Congress recently enacted a return to statutory PAYGO—a budgetary control requiring that the aggregate impact of increases in mandatory spending or reductions in revenue generally be offset.[3] Although this can prevent further deterioration of the fiscal position, it does not deal with the existing imbalance. In February, the President established a commission to identify policies to change the fiscal path and stabilize the debt-to-GDP ratio. Several bipartisan groups have suggested the establishment of a medium-term fiscal goal—such as a ratio of publicly held debt to GDP or of deficit to GDP. While there is no consensus on either the specific target or on the appropriate policy actions to achieve it, these proposals seek to facilitate the policy discussion by setting a benchmark against which to measure future progress.

KEY ASSUMPTIONS IN OUR FEDERAL SIMULATIONS

This update incorporates CBO's most recent baseline projections that were released in January 2010. Table 3 lists the key assumptions incorporated in the Baseline Extended and Alternative simulations for the simulations based on the Trustees' assumptions.

Table 3. Assumptions for Baseline Extended and Alternative Simulations Based on the Trustees' Assumptions for Social Security and Medicare

Model inputs	Baseline Extended	Alternative
Revenue	CBO's January 2010 baseline through 2020; thereafter remains constant at 20.2 percent of GDP (CBO's projection in 2020)	CBO's estimates assuming expiring tax provisions are extended through 2020 and the 2009 AMT exemption amount is indexed to inflation through 2020; thereafter is phased into the 40-year historical average of 18.1 percent of GDP
Social Security spending	CBO's January 2010 baseline through 2020; thereafter based on 2009 Social Security Trustees'	Same as Baseline Extended

Table 3. (Continued)

Model inputs	Baseline Extended	Alternative
	intermediate projections adjusted to reflect wage growth implied in GAO's simulations	
Medicare spending	CBO's January 2010 baseline through 2020 that assumes cuts in physician fees will occur as scheduled under current law[a]; thereafter 2009 Medicare Trustees' intermediate projections that assume per enrollee Medicare spending grows on average 1 percent faster than GDP per capita over the long term	Based on the Centers for Medicare& Medicaid Services' (CMS) alternative scenario that assumes physician fees will remain at current levels (i.e., a physician fee schedule update of 0 percent) instead of being reduced as scheduled under current law[a]
Medicaid spending	CBO's January 2010 baseline through 2020; thereafter CBO's June 2009 long-term projections adjusted to reflect excess cost growth consistent with the 2009 Medicare Trustees' intermediate projections	Same as Baseline Extended
Other mandatory spending	CBO's January 2010 baseline through 2020; thereafter remains constant at 2.2 percent of GDP (implied by CBO's projection in 2020)	Baseline Extended adjusted for extension of certain tax credits through 2020; thereafter is phased back to 2.2 percent of GDP by 2025 (same as Baseline Extended)
Discretionary spending	CBO's January 2010 baseline through 2020; thereafter remains constant at 6.7 percent of GDP (CBO's projection in 2020)	Discretionary spending other than Recovery Act spending increases at the rate of economic growth after 2010 (i.e., remains constant at 8.7 percent of GDP); Recovery Act spending is included but assumed to be temporary

Source: GAO.

Notes: CBO's projections are from *The Budget and Economic Outlook: Fiscal Years 2010 to 2020* (January 2010) and *The Long-Term Budget Outlook* (June 2009). The Trustees' projections are from *The 2009 Annual Report of the Board of Trustees of the Federal Old-Age and Survivors Insurance and Federal Disability Insurance Trust Funds* and *2009 Annual Report of the Boards of Trustees of the Federal Hospital Insurance and Federal Supplementary Medical Insurance Trust Funds* that were both issued on May 12, 2009. We assume that Social Security and Medicare benefits are paid in full regardless of the amounts available in the trust funds.

[a]Under current law, the fees paid for physician services are scheduled to be reduced by about 21 percent in 2010 and additional amounts in subsequent years. Over the past 7 years, in which Congressional action averted scheduled cuts in updates to the physician fee schedule, such updates grew at an average rate of 0.9 percent. Based on historical trends, a 0 percent physician fee update is a conservative assumption for estimating future Medicare spending.

Table 4. Key Assumptions Underlying GAO's Simulations Using CBO's Entitlement Spending Projections

Model inputs	Baseline Extended	Alternative
Social Security spending	CBO's January 2010 baseline through 2020; thereafter based on CBO's August 2009 long-term projections for Social Security. These projections are based on the 2009 Social Security Trustees' demographic projections and CBO's own economic assumptions.	Same as Baseline Extended
Medicare spending	CBO's January 2010 baseline through 2020; thereafter based on CBO's June 2009 long-term projections. Per enrollee Medicare spending grows on average 1.5 percentage points faster than GDP per capita over the long term.	Based on CBO's projections that assume physician payment rates grow with inflation (using the Medicare Economic Index)[a]
Medicaid spending	CBO's January 2010 baseline through 2020; thereafter CBO's June 2009 long-term projections. Per enrollee Medicaid spending grows on average 0.6 percentage points faster than GDP per capita over the long term.	Same as Baseline Extended

Source: GAO.

Notes: CBO's projections are from *CBO's Long-Term Projections for Social Security: 2009 Update* (August 2009) and *The Long-Term Budget Outlook* (June 2009). CBO assumes that full benefits are paid regardless of the amounts available in the trust funds.

[a] Since 2003, inflation in the inputs used for physicians' services measured by the Medicare Economic Index averaged 2.5 percent per year.

In the second set of simulations, we use CBO's projections for Social Security, Medicare, and Medicaid. Table 4 shows the assumptions that differ from those shown in table 3.

Table 5 shows the key economic assumptions that underlie all of our simulations. GDP is held constant across simulations and does not respond to changes in fiscal policy.

Table 5. Key Economic Assumptions Underlying All of GAO's Long-term Federal Simulations

Model inputs	All simulations
Labor: growth in hours worked	2009 Social Security Trustees' intermediate projections
Nonfederal saving: gross saving of the private sector and state and local government sector	Increases gradually over the first 10 years to 18.5 percent of GDP (the average nonfederal saving rate from 1950 to 2009)
Current account balance (percent of GDP)	From 2010 to 2020, 2009 share of GDP plus one-third of any change in gross national saving from 2009; thereafter equal to 2020 nominal level plus one-third of any change in gross national saving from 2009 (that is, a declining share of GDP)
Total factor productivity growth	1.3 percent through 2020 (CBO's January 2010 short-term assumption); 1.4 percent thereafter (long-term average from 1950 to 2009)
Inflation (percent Change in GDP price index)	CBO January 2010 baseline through 2020;1.8 percent thereafter (CBO's projection in 2020)
Interest rate (on publicly held debt)	Rate implied by CBO's January 2010 baseline net interest payment projections through 2020; 5.0 percent thereafter (the rate implied in 2020)

Source: GAO.

We conducted our work from January 2010 to March 2010 in accordance with all sections of GAO's Quality Assurance Framework that are relevant to our objectives. The framework requires that we plan and perform the engagement to obtain sufficient and appropriate evidence to meet our stated objectives and to discuss any limitations in our work. We believe that the information and data obtained, and the analysis conducted, provide a reasonable basis for any findings and conclusions.

End Notes

[1] More information on the different assumptions underlying the two sets of simulations appears on pages 10 and 11.

[2] Our present value calculations take into the account the time value of money by discounting future revenue and spending to reflect the equivalent amount needed today in current dollars. These calculations are sensitive to changes in interest rates, and a portion of the increase in the fiscal gap since our Fall 2009 update is caused by a small decline in our long-term interest rate assumption. More information on interest rates and other economic assumptions in our model can be found on page 12.

[3] For details on the rules governing the implementation of PAYGO, see Public Law 111-139.

In: Federal Budget Outlook and Economic... ISBN: 978-1-61761-769-0
Editors: Michael S. Okada

Chapter 4

THE EFFECTS OF AUTOMATIC STABILIZERS ON THE FEDERAL BUDGET

Congressional Budget Office

In March 2010, the Congressional Budget Office (CBO) released its most recent baseline projections of federal revenues, outlays, and budget balances for the next 10 years.[1] For those projections, CBO assumed the continuation of current laws and policies that affect taxes and mandatory spending programs and extrapolated the growth of discretionary spending by using projected rates of inflation. CBO estimated in March that the baseline budget deficit will total $463billion in 2014, compared with a deficit of $1.4 trillion in 2009. The deficit was 9.9 percent of gross domestic product (GDP) in 2009—the largest share in more than half a century. By the end of 2014, CBO projects, the deficit will amount to 2.6percent of GDP if current laws and policies remain in place.

Fluctuations in the budget deficit are influenced by legislation that governs taxation and spending and by the automatic responses of revenues and outlays to developments in the economy and other factors. This chapter focuses on a component of the latter group—the automatic stabilizers—that reflect cyclical movements in real (inflation-adjusted) output and unemployment.[2] During cyclical slowdowns and recessions, the economy grows more slowly than it could if it achieved its potential, andrevenue growth declines automatically as well. In addition, some spending—for example, to pay unemployment insurance claims or to provide federal nutrition benefits—

automatically increases. Those automatic reductions in revenues and increases in outlays help to bolster the economy, but they also temporarily increase the budget deficit. The opposite occurs when there are upturns in the business cycle; that is, automatic stabilizers tend to shrink as the economy moves toward its potential output. (For a discussion of automatic stabilizers and their uses, see the appendix.)

In 2009, CBO estimates, automatic stabilizers added the equivalent of 1.9 percent of potential GDP to the deficit, an amount substantially greater than the 0.3 percent added in 2008.[3] According to CBO's baseline projections, the contribution of automatic stabilizers to the budget deficit will be roughly 2.3 percent of potential GDP in 2010 and 2.5 percent of potential GDP in 2011. The contribution will then decrease to 2.0 percent in 2012, 1.0 percent in 2013, and 0.2 percent in 2014 (see Tables 1 and2). The pattern arises because CBO expects that GDP will remain well below its potential in 2010 and 2011 but that the gap between actual and potential GDP will narrow in 2012 and 2013 and be nearly gone by 2014. Diminished tax revenues account for the bulk of the budgetary impact of automatic stabilizers. The reduction in revenues because of the GDP gap will average about 1.8 percent of potential GDP over the 2009–2012 period, CBO estimates.

The budget balance without automatic stabilizers is an estimate of what the surplus or deficit would be if GDP was at its potential, the unemployment rate was at a corresponding level, and all other factors were unchanged. Such a budget measure has several applications. For example, some analysts use such a measure to discern underlying trends in government saving or dissaving (that is, trends in surpluses or deficits). Others use it to approximate whether the short-run influence of the budget on aggregate demand and on the growth of real output is positive or negative. More generally, the measure helps analysts estimate the extent to which changes in the budget balance are caused by movements of the business cycle and thus are likely to prove temporary rather than long-lasting.

Under CBO's baseline assumptions, the budget deficit without automatic stabilizers (previously called the cyclically adjusted deficit by CBO and sometimes called the structural deficit) would constitute 6.5 percent of potential GDP in 2010, down from 7.5 percent in 2009. CBO projects that the baseline deficit without automatic stabilizers will shrink further in the next two years, to 3.7percent in 2011 and 1.9 percent in 2012, before increasing again, to 2.1 percent in 2013 and 2.5 percent in 2014 (see Figure 1).

Table 1.The Budget Deficit or Surplus With and Without Automatic Stabilizers and Related Series in Billions of Dollars, 1962 to 2014

	Budget Deficit (-) or Surplus With Automatic Stabilizers	– Automatic = Stabilizers	Budget Deficit (-) or Surplus Without Automatic Stabilizers	Budget Revenues and Outlays Without Automatic Stabilizers		GDP Gap[a]	Unemployment Gap (Percent)[b]
				Revenues	Outlays		
1962	-7	-2	-5	101	106	-7	0.5
1963	-5	-2	-3	108	111	-6	0.1
1964	-6	1	-7	112	119	3	-0.1
1965	-1	3	-5	114	119	10	-0.7
1966	-4	11	-14	122	136	33	-1.7
1967	-9	10	-19	141	160	29	-2.0
1968	-25	8	-34	147	180	23	-2.0
1969	3	11	-8	179	187	26	-2.4
1970	-3	3	-6	192	198	3	-1.9
1971	-23	-4	-19	191	210	-15	-0.2
1972	-23	-1	-22	209	231	-5	-0.1
1973	-15	12	-27	220	247	39	-0.9
1974	-6	10	-16	255	272	28	-1.2
1975	-53	-17	-36	293	329	-56	1.2

Table 1. (Continued)

	Budget Deficit (-) or Surplus With Automatic Stabilizers	– Automatic = Stabilizers	Budget Deficit (-) or Surplus Without Automatic Stabilizers	Budget Revenues and Outlays Without Automatic Stabilizers		GDP Gap[a]	Unemployment Gap (Percent)[b]
				Revenues	Outlays		
1976	-74	-20	-54	313	367	-53	1.8
1977	-54	-11	-43	364	406	-28	1.1
1978	-59	2	-61	398	459	7	*
1979	-41	10	-50	456	506	26	-0.4
1980	-74	-14	-60	528	588	-47	0.6
1981	-79	-21	-58	615	673	-52	1.2
1982	-128	-56	-72	665	737	-188	3.0
1983	-208	-74	-133	663	797	-230	4.1
1984	-185	-25	-160	689	850	-76	1.8
1985	-212	-13	-199	744	943	-35	1.2
1986	-221	-9	-213	775	987	-20	1.0
1987	-150	-13	-137	866	1,003	-36	0.4
1988	-155	6	-162	905	1,067	20	-0.3
1989	-153	21	-174	973	1,147	58	-0.7
1990	-221	14	-235	1,020	1,255	28	-0.5
1991	-269	-51	-219	1,100	1,318	-161	0.8
1992	-290	-69	-221	1,150	1,371	-171	1.7

Table 1. (Continued)

	Budget Deficit (-) or Surplus With Automatic Stabilizers	– Automatic = Stabilizers	Budget Deficit (-) or Surplus Without Automatic Stabilizers	Budget Revenues and Outlays Without Automatic Stabilizers		GDP Gap[a]	Unemployment Gap (Percent)[b]
				Revenues	Outlays		
1993	-255	-57	-198	1,203	1,402	-140	1.5
1994	-203	-38	-165	1,293	1,458	-83	0.9
1995	-164	-27	-137	1,378	1,515	-77	0.3
1996	-107	-29	-78	1,481	1,559	-72	0.3
1997	-22	5	-27	1,575	1,602	28	*
1998	69	38	31	1,688	1,657	100	-0.5
1999	126	86	39	1,747	1,708	230	-0.7
2000	236	133	103	1,900	1,797	337	-1.0
2001	128	81	47	1,915	1,867	155	-0.7
2002	-158	-17	-141	1,861	2,002	-57	0.7
2003	-378	-65	-313	1,837	2,150	-186	1.0
2004	-413	-36	-377	1,911	2,288	-82	0.6
2005	-318	-7	-312	2,160	2,472	-5	0.2
2006	-248	14	-262	2,398	2,660	32	-0.3
2007	-161	0	-161	2,574	2,735	-26	-0.5
2008	-459	-47	-412	2,565	2,976	-169	0.3
2009	-1,413	-282	-1,131	2,326	3,457	-932	3.5

Table 1. (Continued)

	Budget Deficit (-) or Surplus With Automatic Stabilizers	– Automatic = Stabilizers	Budget Deficit (-) or Surplus Without Automatic Stabilizers	Budget Revenues and Outlays Without Automatic Stabilizers		GDP Gap[a]	Unemployment Gap (Percent)[b]
				Revenues	Outlays		
2010	-1,368	-351	-1,018	2,450	3,467	-983	5.2
2011c	-996	-403	-593	3,011	3,604	-970	4.8
2012c	-642	-331	-310	3,256	3,566	-696	3.4
2013c	-525	-163	-362	3,368	3,730	-301	1.7
2014c	-463	-29	-433	3,498	3,931	-22	0.4

Sources: Congressional Budget Office; Office of Management and Budget.

Notes: Automatic stabilizers are automatic changes in revenues and outlays that are attributable to cyclical movements in real (inflation-adjusted) output and unemployment.

GDP = gross domestic product; * = between -0.05 percent and 0.05 percent.

a. The GDP gap equals actual (or projected) GDP minus potential GDP (the quantity of output that corresponds to a high rate of use of labor and capital).

b. The unemployment gap equals the actual (or projected) rate of unemployment minus the natural rate of unemployment, which is the rateof unemployment arising from all sources except fluctuations in aggregate demand.

c. Projected using CBO's baseline assumptions.

Table 2. The Budget Deficit or Surplus With and Without Automatic Stabilizers and Related Series as a Percentage of Potential GDP, 1962 to 2014

	Budget Deficit (-) or Surplus With Automatic Stabilizers	– Automatic = Stabilizers	Budget Deficit (-) or Surplus Without Automatic Stabilizers	Budget Revenues and Outlays Without Automatic Stabilizers		GDP Gap[a]	Unemployment Gap (Percent)[b]
				Revenues	Outlays		
1962	-1.2	-0.4	-0.9	17.6	18.5	-1.1	0.5
1963	-0.8	-0.3	-0.5	17.9	18.4	-1.1	0.1
1964	-0.9	0.2	-1.1	17.5	18.6	0.4	-0.1
1965	-0.2	0.5	-0.7	16.8	17.6	1.5	-0.7
1966	-0.5	1.5	-2.0	16.9	18.9	4.6	-1.7
1967	-1.1	1.3	-2.4	18.1	20.5	3.8	-2.0
1968	-3.0	1.0	-4.0	17.4	21.3	2.7	-2.0
1969	0.4	1.2	-0.8	19.4	20.3	2.9	-2.4
1970	-0.3	0.3	-0.6	19.0	19.6	0.3	-1.9
1971	-2.1	-0.4	-1.7	17.5	19.2	-1.4	-0.2
1972	-2.0	-0.1	-1.9	17.7	19.5	-0.4	-0.1
1973	-1.2	1.0	-2.1	17.3	19.5	3.1	-0.9
1974	-0.4	0.7	-1.2	18.1	19.3	2.0	-1.2
1975	-3.3	-1.1	-2.2	18.1	20.3	-3.5	1.2

Table 2. (Continued)

	Budget Deficit (-) or Surplus With Automatic Stabilizers	– Automatic = Stabilizers	Budget Deficit (-) or Surplus Without Automatic Stabilizers	Budget Revenues and Outlays Without Automatic Stabilizers		GDP Gap[a]	Unemployment Gap (Percent)[b]
				Revenues	Outlays		
1976	-4.1	-1.1	-3.0	17.5	20.5	-3.0	1.8
1977	-2.7	-0.6	-2.1	18.2	20.3	-1.4	1.1
1978	-2.7	0.1	-2.8	18.0	20.8	0.3	*
1979	-1.6	0.4	-2.0	18.4	20.4	1.0	-0.4
1980	-2.7	-0.5	-2.2	19.1	21.2	-1.7	0.6
1981	-2.5	-0.7	-1.9	19.8	21.7	-1.7	1.2
1982	-3.8	-1.6	-2.1	19.5	21.6	-5.5	3.0
1983	-5.7	-2.0	-3.6	18.1	21.7	-6.3	4.1
1984	-4.7	-0.6	-4.1	17.6	21.7	-1.9	1.8
1985	-5.1	-0.3	-4.8	17.8	22.6	-0.8	1.2
1986	-5.0	-0.2	-4.8	17.5	22.3	-0.4	1.0
1987	-3.2	-0.3	-2.9	18.5	21.4	-0.8	0.4
1988	-3.1	0.1	-3.2	18.1	21.4	0.4	-0.3
1989	-2.9	0.4	-3.3	18.2	21.5	1.1	-0.7
1990	-3.9	0.2	-4.1	17.9	22.0	0.5	-0.5
1991	-4.4	-0.8	-3.6	18.0	21.6	-2.6	0.8
1992	-4.5	-1.1	-3.4	17.9	21.4	-2.7	1.7

Table 2. (Continued)

	Budget Deficit (-) or Surplus With Automatic Stabilizers	– Automatic = Stabilizers	Budget Deficit (-) or Surplus Without Automatic Stabilizers	Budget Revenues and Outlays Without Automatic Stabilizers		GDP Gap[a]	Unemployment Gap (Percent)[b]
				Revenues	Outlays		
1993	-3.8	-0.8	-2.9	17.9	20.8	-2.1	1.5
1994	-2.9	-0.5	-2.3	18.3	20.7	-1.2	0.9
1995	-2.2	-0.4	-1.8	18.6	20.4	-1.0	0.3
1996	-1.4	-0.4	-1.0	19.0	20.0	-0.9	0.3
1997	-0.3	0.1	-0.3	19.2	19.6	0.3	*
1998	0.8	0.4	0.4	19.7	19.4	1.2	-0.5
1999	1.4	1.0	0.4	19.5	19.0	2.6	-0.7
2000	2.5	1.4	1.1	20.0	19.0	3.6	-1.0
2001	1.3	0.8	0.5	19.0	18.5	1.5	-0.7
2002	-1.5	-0.2	-1.3	17.6	18.9	-0.5	0.7
2003	-3.4	-0.6	-2.8	16.5	19.3	-1.7	1.0
2004	-3.5	-0.3	-3.2	16.2	19.4	-0.7	0.6
2005	-2.6	-0.1	-2.5	17.3	19.9	*	0.2
2006	-1.9	0.1	-2.0	18.2	20.2	0.2	-0.3
2007	-1.2	*	-1.2	18.5	19.6	-0.2	-0.5
2008	-3.1	-0.3	-2.8	17.6	20.4	-1.2	0.3
2009	-9.3	-1.9	-7.5	15.3	22.8	-6.1	3.5

Table 2. (Continued)

	Budget Deficit (-) or Surplus With Automatic Stabilizers	– Automatic = Stabilizers	Budget Deficit (-) or Surplus Without Automatic Stabilizers	Budget Revenues and Outlays Without Automatic Stabilizers		GDP Gap[a]	Unemployment Gap (Percent)[b]
				Revenues	Outlays		
2010c	-8.8	-2.3	-6.5	15.7	22.3	-6.3	5.2
2011c	-6.2	-2.5	-3.7	18.9	22.6	-6.1	4.8
2012c	-3.9	-2.0	-1.9	19.8	21.7	-4.2	3.4
2013c	-3.1	-1.0	-2.1	19.8	22.0	-1.8	1.7
2014c	-2.6	-0.2	-2.5	19.8	22.3	-0.1	0.4

Sources: Congressional Budget Office; Office of Management and Budget.

Notes: Automatic stabilizers are automatic changes in revenues and outlays that are attributable to cyclical movements in real (inflation-adjusted) output and unemployment. Potential GDP is the quantity of output that corresponds to a high rate of use of labor and capital.

GDP = gross domestic product; * = between -0.05 percent and 0.05 percent.

a. The GDP gap equals actual (or projected) GDP minus potential GDP.

b. The unemployment gap equals the actual (or projected) rate of unemployment minus the natural rate of unemployment, which is the rateof unemployment arising from all sources except fluctuations in aggregate demand.

c. Projected using CBO's baseline assumptions.

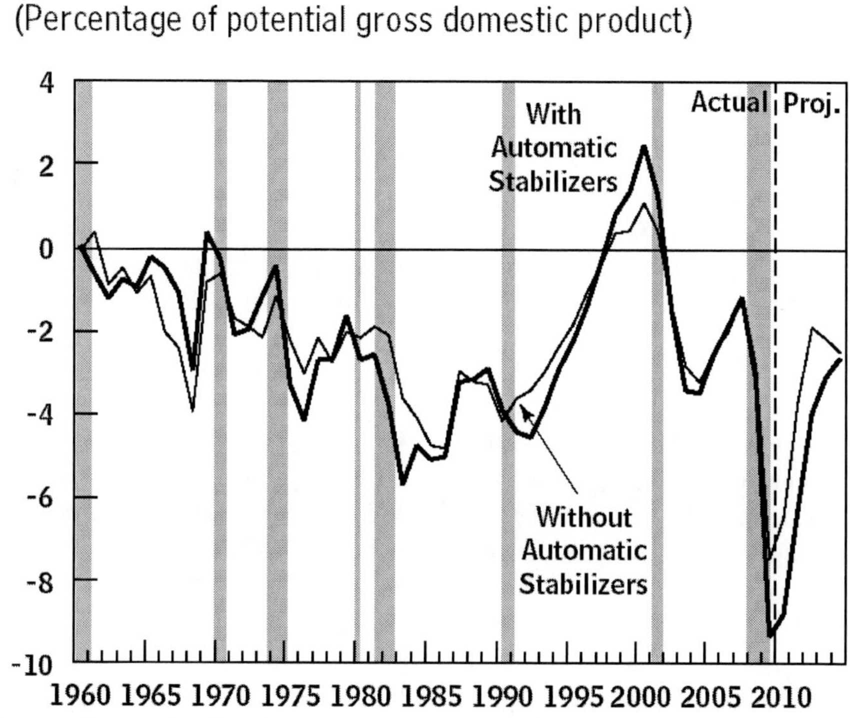

Sources: Congressional Budget Office; Office of Management and Budget.

Notes: Automatic stabilizers are automatic changes in revenues and outlays that are attributable to cyclical movements in real (inflation-adjusted) output and unemployment.

Potential gross domestic product is the quantity of output that corresponds to a high rate of use of labor and capital.

The shaded vertical bars indicate periods of recession, which extend from the peak of a business cycle to its trough. The National Bureau of Economic Research establishes dates on which recessions begin and end but has not yet done so for the end of the most recent recession, which is shown here as having ended in the second quarter of 2009.

The dashed vertical line separates actual from projected data.

Figure 1. Two Measures of Budget Deficits and Surpluses

The decrease in the deficit without automatic stabilizers from 2009 to 2010, as a percentage of potential GDP, results from several factors. Revenues are boosted by a jump in receipts to the Treasury from the Federal Reserve and from individual income taxes. The unusual increase in receipts from the central bank results from a shift in the Federal Reserve's portfolio to longer-term, riskier, and thus higher-yielding investments in support of the housing market and the broader economy. Receipts from individual income taxes rise relative to potential GDP in part because of real bracket creep (in which growth in inflation-adjusted income causes more income to be taxed in higher tax brackets) and increases in taxable pension distributions and in distributions from individual retirement accounts. In addition, total spending rises very little in nominal terms (and thus declines as a share of GDP) because substantial reductions in outlays for the Troubled Asset Relief Program and for federal assistance to Fannie Mae and Freddie Mac offset most of the increase in other spending.

For 2011, the projected decline in the deficit without automatic stabilizers as a percentage of potential GDP results largely from the scheduled expiration in December 2010 of tax cuts enacted in 2001 and 2003 and from the additional taxes that will be paid in 2011 because, under current law, many more households will be subject to the alternative minimum tax. The projected further decrease in the deficit without automatic stabilizers for 2012 occurs because of additional revenue gains attributable to the expiration of tax cuts in 2010, other factors that raise effective tax rates, and a waning of spending under the American Recovery and Reinvestment Act of 2009.[4] The projected increases in the deficit without automatic stabilizers in 2013 and 2014 can be attributed to projected growth in interest payments, which amounts to 0.3 percent of potential GDP each year. Noninterest spending without automatic stabilizers does not change as a percentage of potential GDP.

APPENDIX: MEASURING THE BUDGETARYEFFECTS OF AUTOMATICSTABILIZER

The size of the budget deficit is influenced by policy changes and by the automatic responses of revenues and outlays to economic developments and other factors. In addition to the effects of changes in real (inflation-adjusted) output and unemployment—which are most pronounced during recessions—key economic factors include changes in the long-term (trend) growth rate of output and income, movements in the proportion of income subject to taxation and the distribution of that income, and variations in interest rates and in the pace of inflation.

This chapter measures the effect on the budget of automatic stabilizers, which are automatic changes in revenues and outlays that are driven by the business cycle. Those stabilizers mitigate the decline of real income in recessions and dampen its growth in booms. The Congressional Budget Office (CBO) estimates that in fiscal year 2000, automatic stabilizers contributed to the budget surplus an amount that was equal to 1.4 percent of potential gross domestic product (GDP), indicating that the strength of the economy was significantly augmenting the budget surplus. By 2002, the automatic stabilizers' contribution had turned negative, in CBO's estimation, because the economy was operating below its potential and adding to the budget deficit. Significant negative contributions persisted through 2004. From 2005 through 2007, the effects of the automatic stabilizers were quite small because the economy was close to its potential. More recently, they have contributed much more to the deficit as the economy has operated significantly below its potential.

CBO arrives at its estimate of the deficit without automatic stabilizers by removing their effects from the total budget deficit. For revenues, CBO estimates taxable income as though overall output equaled its potential, and it translates the difference between that income and actual income into cyclical losses in revenue. For outlays, CBO estimates what unemployment would be if output were at its potential, and it translates the difference between that number and actual unemployment into cyclical increases in spending for unemployment insurance benefits and other income support programs.

Economic factors (such as inflation and interest rates) that are not directly cyclical and are therefore not removed from the estimates presented in this chapter also have automatic effects on the budget. For example, a higher rate of inflation would boost the dollar value of taxable income and thus increase federal tax receipts. Because interest rates also are affected by inflation, federal interest payments would be higher. Spending that is indexed for inflation (Social Security benefits, for example) also would increase. However, such budget effects of factors other than changes in real output and unemployment are not analyzed here.

In a few cases, CBO's analysis of automatic stabilizers attempts to adjust for the budgetary effects of economic factors whose connection to cyclical fluctuations has varied over time. For example, fluctuations in tax receipts from realized capital gains appear to have moved more closely with the business cycle recently than in earlier cycles; CBO's estimates of automatic stabilizers incorporate the changing relationship over time. Similarly, compensation bonuses, which tend to be concentrated among taxpayers in relatively high tax brackets and which thus affect the effective tax rate on total wages and salaries, seem to have become more cyclical, and that too is reflected in the estimates. Changes over time in the cyclical differences between taxable corporate profits and corporate profits as measured in the national incomeandproduct accounts also are accounted for in CBO's calculation of the budgetary effects of the automatic stabilizers.

Despite adjustments to revenues and outlays for the automatic effects of the business cycle, the deficit without automatic stabilizers can exhibit apparently regular cyclical characteristics—such as increases during times of recession and early recovery. In part, that pattern reflects policy responses to recessions. The government often chooses to stimulate a weakening economy by cutting taxes or increasing government spending, both of which increase the deficit (or reduce the surplus). The American Recovery and Reinvestment Act of 2009; the Troubled Asset Relief Program (TARP); and the Housing and Economic Recovery Act of 2008, which led to federal conservatorship of Fannie Mae and Freddie Mac, were deficit-raising measures enacted to directly or indirectly address the recent recession. Such responses to recessions are not "automatic," however, because they require legislation, and their budget effects thus are not part of the automatic stabilizers. Another reason that the deficit without automatic stabilizers can exhibit residual cyclical movements is that estimates of the budgetary impact of automatic stabilizers might only partly remove the effects of factors (such as large fluctuations in the stock market) that have not had a sufficiently regular relationship to business cycles to be viewed as mostly cyclical.

In its annual reports on the budget and the economy, CBO presents "rules of thumb" that describe how the budget balance would differ if certain economic outcomes were different than projected.[5] Those estimates attempt to capture the effects of sustained changes in the rate of growth of GDP and other economic variables, whereas the estimates in this chapter are meant to filter out temporary fluctuations that are attributable to automatic stabilizers.

End Notes

[1] See Congressional Budget Office, *An Analysis of the President's Budgetary Proposals for Fiscal Year 2011* (March 2010).

[2] This is the same concept CBO previously referred to as the cyclical contribution to the budget balance. For a description of methodology for estimating automatic stabilizers that is similar to CBO's methodology, see Darrel Cohen and Glenn Follette, "The Automatic Fiscal Stabilizers: Quietly Doing Their Thing," in *Economic Policy Review*, Federal Reserve Bank of New York, vol. 6, no. 1 (April 2000), pp. 35–68.

[3] That and subsequent calculations in this chapter involve potential, rather than actual, GDP because potential GDP excludes fluctuations that are attributable to the business cycle.

Potential GDP is the quantity of output that corresponds to a high rate of use of labor and capital.

[4] The expiration of the tax cuts will result in more revenues in 2012 than in 2011 primarily because the resulting higher tax rates will affect withheld taxes for all four quarters of fiscal year 2012, compared with three quarters of fiscal year 2011.

[5] See Congressional Budget Office, *The Budget and Economic Outlook: Fiscal Years 2010 to 2020* (January 2010), Appendix C.

In: Federal Budget Outlook and Economic... ISBN: 978-1-61761-769-0
Editors: Michael S. Okada

Chapter 5

THE BUDGET RESOLUTION AND SPENDING LEGISLATION

Megan Suzanne Lynch

SUMMARY

The budget resolution sets forth aggregate levels of spending, revenue, and public debt. It is not intended to establish details of spending or revenue policy and does not provide levels of spending for specific agencies or programs. Instead, its purpose is to create enforceable parameters within which Congress can consider legislation dealing with spending and revenue.

The spending policies in the budget resolution encompass two types of spending legislation: discretionary spending and direct (mandatory) spending. Discretionary spending is controlled through the appropriations process. Appropriations legislation is considered each fiscal year and provides funding for numerous programs such as national defense, education, and homeland security. Direct spending, alternately, is provided for in legislation outside of appropriations acts. Direct spending programs are typically established in permanent law and continue in effect until such time as revised or terminated by another law.

The budget resolution establishes congressional priorities by dividing spending among the 20 major functional categories of the federal budget. These 20 categories do not correspond to the committee system by which

Congress operates, and as a result these spending levels must be "crosswalked" to the House and Senate committees having jurisdiction over both discretionary and direct spending. These amounts are known as 302(a) allocations and hold committees accountable for staying within the spending limits established by the budget resolution.

Each Appropriations Committee is responsible for subdividing its 302(a) allocation among its 12 subcommittees. These allocations, referred to as 302(b) subdivisions, establish the maximum amount that each of the 12 appropriations bills can spend.

It is inevitable that Members will consider the impact on particular programs or agencies when they consider a budget resolution. While the budget resolution does not allocate funds among specific agencies or programs, congressional assumptions or desires underlying the amounts set forth in the functional categories are frequently communicated through the budget resolution. Report language accompanying the budget resolution, as well as certain provisions in the budget resolution, can sometimes express non-binding programmatic assumptions and desires.

Budget resolutions also often include procedural provisions such as reserve funds or reconciliation instructions. These provisions may also reflect underlying program assumptions or desires of Congress.

INTRODUCTION

The Constitution grants Congress the power of the purse and provides that "No money shall be drawn from the Treasury, but in Consequence of Appropriations made by Law."[1] It does not, however, establish any specific procedures by which Congress must consider spending legislation. Instead, Congress has developed rules and practices that govern consideration of spending and other budgetary legislation under each chamber's constitutional authority to " ... determine the Rules of its Proceedings."[2]

It is under this authority that the procedures in the Congressional Budget Act of 1974 were created.[3] The Congressional Budget Act established the basic framework that is used today for congressional consideration of budget and fiscal policy. It provides for the annual adoption of a concurrent resolution on the budget as a mechanism for coordinating congressional budgetary decision making.[4]

The budget resolution creates enforceable parameters with which spending, revenue, and debt legislation must be consistent. It is not a law. It is not signed by the President nor can it be vetoed. Instead, its purpose is to establish a framework within which Congress considers legislation dealing with spending and revenue.

The budget resolution is not intended to establish details of spending or revenue policy. Instead, details of such policy are to be included in legislation reported from the committees with legislative jurisdiction subsequent to the adoption of the budget resolution. All spending or revenue legislation reported from legislative committees, however, is expected to be consistent with the levels and priorities agreed to in the budget resolution.

The spending policies in the budget resolution encompass two types of spending legislation: discretionary spending and direct (or mandatory) spending. Discretionary spending is controlled through the appropriations process. Appropriations legislation is considered annually for the fiscal year beginning October 1. Appropriations legislation provides funding for numerous activities such as national defense, education, and homeland security, as well as general government operations.[5]

Direct spending, alternately, is provided for in legislation outside of appropriations acts. Direct spending programs are typically established in permanent law that continue in effect until such time as they are revised or terminated by another law. The actual annual cost of direct spending is not determined by Congress. It is instead dictated by formulas within the legislation providing for the program. The overall cost of a program depends on the eligibility requirements and benefits set forth in the legislation. These criteria determine who will be eligible to receive benefits and how much benefit they will receive. Only by altering these formulas can Congress adjust how much money will be spent.

THE BUDGET RESOLUTION

Content

The budget resolution sets forth levels for new budget authority, outlays, revenue, and public debt for the budget year and four outyears.[6] The levels in the budget resolution deal with aggregates, not programmatic spending details. Assumptions concerning some major programs may be discussed in the reports accompanying the budget resolution, but these assumptions are not in the form of legislative language and are not binding on the committee of jurisdiction.

Rather than including levels of spending for specific agencies or programs, the budget resolution establishes congressional priorities by dividing spending among the 20 major functional categories of the federal budget.[7] These 20 functional categories do not correspond to the committee system by which Congress operates. As a result, the spending levels in the 20 functional categories are allocated, or "crosswalked," to the House and Senate committees having jurisdiction over discretionary spending (appropriations committees) and direct spending (legislative committees). These "crosswalked" totals appear in the joint explanatory statement of the conference report on the budget resolution and are referred to as 302(a) allocations.[8] These 302(a) amounts hold committees accountable for staying within the spending limits established by the budget resolution.

Programmatic Assumptions

It is inevitable that Members will consider the impact on particular programs or agencies when they consider a budget resolution. Each committee is required to submit its "views and estimates" with information on the preferences and legislative plans of that committee regarding budget matters to help the Budget Committee determine spending levels for each of the functional categories.

While the budget resolution does not allocate funds among specific agencies or programs, assumptions underlying the amounts set forth in the functional categories are frequently discussed in the reports accompanying the budget resolution. For example, the committee print accompanying the budget resolution for FY2009 included the following language:

> The Committee-reported resolution assumes approximately $2 billion for the Department of Energy's Energy Efficiency and Renewable Energy program. The funding level is $738 million above the President's request and would accommodate significant increases for programs such as wind, solar, geothermal, biomass and biorefinery R&D, hydrogen, and vehicle/building technologies. This funding level would also provide $450 million for the Weatherization Assistance Program, a program which was zeroed out in the President's budget.[9]

Report language, however, is not binding on the committees with jurisdiction over spending and revenue.

In addition to report language, certain provisions often included in the budget resolution may indicate programmatic assumptions or desires. Budget resolutions frequently include "Sense of the Congress" language expressing the assumptions or desires of one or both chambers for certain programs to receive priority in funding. For example, the budget resolution for FY2010 included language concerning the sense of the Congress on Great Lakes restoration:

> It is the sense of the Congress that this resolution recognizes the need to address significant and long-standing problems affecting the major large scale aquatic, estuarine, and coastal ecosystems nationwide. This resolution includes funding for a new interagency initiative to address such regional ecosystems. It also includes funding to work with Great Lakes States, tribes, local communities, and organizations to more effectively address issues prioritized in the Great Lakes Regional Collaborative. This initiative could address issues such as invasive species, habitat restoration and conservation, non-point source pollution, and contaminated sediment. The resolution also supports the President's proposal to use outcome-oriented performance goals and measures to target the most significant problems and track progress in addressing these ecosystems.[10]

Budget resolutions may also include "Policy" statements.[11] These statements sometimes include language indicating that spending levels in the budget resolution assume certain policies will be carried out. For example,

> It is the policy of this resolution that ...
>
> (5) TRICARE fees for military retirees under the age of 65 should not be increased as the President's budget proposes;[12]

Neither "Sense of the Congress" provisions nor "Policy" statements are binding on the committees with jurisdiction over spending and revenue.

Budget resolutions often include procedural provisions, such as reserve funds or reconciliation instructions. These provisions often indicate underlying program assumptions or desires of Congress. (Further information on reserve funds and reconciliation instructions is provided below.)

Formulation of the Budget and the Budget Cycle

Federal budgeting is a cyclical activity. The President submits a budget request to Congress early in the calendar year. Congressional committees then hold hearings where they hear testimony from OMB officials, presidential advisors, and agencies who defend the President's budget recommendations.

Committees then submit their "views and estimates" to the Budget Committee of their respective chamber. A committee's "views and estimates" provide the Budget Committees with information on the preferences and legislative plans of that committee regarding budget matters within its jurisdiction. House and Senate Budget Committees then consider and report a budget resolution.

The Congressional Budget Act establishes a timetable for the consideration of budgetary legislation. This timetable provides various target dates that reflect when certain actions typically occur. Once the budget resolution is adopted, chambers may consider appropriations bills and any other spending and revenue legislation consistent with the budget resolution.

Table 1. Congressional Budget Process Timetable

Deadline	Action to be completed
First Monday in February[13]	President submits his budget.
February 15	CBO submits report to Budget Committees.
Six weeks after President's budget is submitted	Committees submit views and estimates to Budget Committees.
April 1	Senate Budget Committee reports concurrent resolution on the budget.
April 15	Congress completes action on concurrent resolution on the budget.
May 15	Annual appropriations bills may be considered in the House.
June 10	House Appropriations Committee reports last annual appropriations bill.
June 15	Congress completes action on reconciliation legislation.
June 30	House completes action on regular appropriations bills.
October 1	Fiscal year begins.

Source: Sec. 300 of the Budget Act.

DISCRETIONARY SPENDING

The 302(a) allocations made to the House and Senate Appropriations Committees reflect their jurisdiction over all discretionary spending. These allocations hold the appropriations committees accountable for staying within the spending limits established by the budget resolution. In recent years, budget resolutions have also sometimes included explicit spending limits on discretionary spending.[14]

Both the House and Senate Appropriations Committees have 12 subcommittees. Each of these subcommittees is responsible for reporting one regular appropriations bill. Sometimes these bills are packaged together in what is referred to as an omnibus appropriations act.

Once an Appropriations Committee has received its 302(a) allocation, it then subdivides the committee allocation among its subcommittees as soon as practicable after the budget resolution has been adopted. These suballocations are known as 302(b) subdivisions.[15] The appropriations committees may make allocations among subcommittees, even if they do not correspond with the levels set forth in the functional categories of the budget resolution. Section 302(c) of the Budget Act provides a point of order against the consideration of any appropriations measures before the Appropriations Committee reports its subdivisions.

The appropriations committees are then required to report these subdivisions to their respective chambers. The appropriations committees may revise the 302(b) subdivisions anytime during the appropriations process to reflect actions taken on spending legislation. If an appropriations committee does adjust the subdivisions among subcommittees, it must inform its respective chamber of the new levels by issuing a new 302(b) subdivision report.

After extensive hearings, each of the subcommittees reports one of the regular appropriations bills to its respective full appropriations committee. Then, the full Appropriations Committee reports the bill to its respective chamber.

Section 302(f) of the Budget Act prohibits consideration of any measure or amendment that would cause the 302(a) or 302(b) allocations to be exceeded. Since appropriations subcommittees usually report their bills at the maximum level of spending, amendments offered to the appropriations bill on the floor are often vulnerable to being ruled out of order since they would cause the spending to exceed the 302(b).[16]

This rule, combined with other rules and practices, makes it difficult to rearrange spending priorities within an appropriations bill through amendments on the floor. A separate amendment (or amendments) to reduce spending would need to be agreed upon prior to, or in conjunction with, one that would increase spending for an agency or program in order to offset that increase.[17]

DIRECT SPENDING

House and Senate legislative committees also receive 302(a) allocations that reflect their jurisdiction over direct spending programs. Any legislation reported by these committees must be consistent with these allocations.[18] As with discretionary spending, Section 302(f) prohibits the consideration of any measure or amendment that would cause the 302(a) allocation to be exceeded.

Reconciliation

Points of order can effectively limit spending that results from appropriations acts or new entitlement legislation to levels consistent with the budget resolution, but are not an effective control on spending that results from existing laws providing direct spending. As a result, Congress has established the reconciliation process as a way to instruct committees to develop legislation to change current revenue or direct spending laws so that these programs conform with policies established in the budget resolution.[19]

The reconciliation process is an optional two-stage process in which instructions are included in the budget resolution. Reconciliation instructions are in the form of a directive to a specific committee to recommend legislative changes. These instructions are specific and include (1) the committee responsible for making the change, (2) the dollar amount of the change, and (3) the period over which this change should be measured. Reconciliation instructions also include a deadline for the committee to submit such recommendations. For example, the budget resolution for FY2006 included the following reconciliation instruction:

> (a) SUBMISSIONS TO SLOW THE GROWTH IN MANDATORY SPENDING- (1) Not later than September 16, 2005, the House committees

named in paragraph (2) shall submit their recommendations to the House Committee on the Budget. After receiving those recommendations, the House Committee on the Budget shall report to the House a reconciliation bill carrying out all such recommendations without any substantive revision.

(2) INSTRUCTIONS-

(A) COMMITTEE ON AGRICULTURE- The House Committee on Agriculture shall report changes in laws within its jurisdiction sufficient to reduce the level of direct spending for that committee by $173,000,000 in outlays for fiscal year 2006 and $3,000,000,000 in outlays for the period of fiscal years 2006 through 2010.[20]

Many changes in direct spending programs have been a result of reconciliation legislation. For example, the instructions in the above example resulted in Title I of the Deficit Reduction Act of 2005 (P.L. 109-171), a reconciliation act. Other titles of that measure included language to make changes in Medicare (Title V), Medicaid and SCHIP (Title VI), and LIHEAP (Title IX). Similarly, reconciliation acts in other years have included titles making changes in diverse direct spending programs as well.

The reconciliation process begins when Congress includes reconciliation instructions in a budget resolution directing one or more committees to recommend changes in current law to achieve the levels of direct spending, revenues, or the debt limit agreed to in the budget resolution. Committees respond to these instructions by drafting legislative language to meet their specified targets. The legislative language recommended by committees is packaged "without any substantive revision" into one or more reconciliation bills by the House and Senate Budget Committees. If only a single committee is instructed to recommend reconciliation changes then those changes are reported directly to its respective chamber. Once reported, reconciliation legislation is considered under special procedures on the House and Senate floor.

RESERVE FUNDS

Spending allocations may be revised subsequent to the adoption of the budget resolution if provided for in the budget resolution. Congress frequently includes provisions referred to as "reserve funds" in the annual budget resolution, which provide the chairs of the House and Senate Budget Committees the authority to adjust the committee spending allocations if certain conditions are met. Typically these conditions consist of legislation dealing with a particular policy being reported by the appropriate committee or an amendment dealing with that policy being offered on the floor. Once this action has taken place, the Budget Committee chairman submits the adjustment to his respective chamber.

Reserve funds frequently require that the net budgetary impact of the specified legislation be deficit neutral. Deficit-neutral reserve funds provide that a committee may report legislation with spending in excess of its allocations, but require the excess amounts be "offset" by equivalent amounts. The Budget Committee chairman may then increase the committee spending allocations by the appropriate amounts to prevent a point of order under Section 302 of the Budget Act. For example, the budget resolution for FY2009 included the following language providing for a deficit-neutral reserve fund concerning San Joaquin River restoration and Navajo nation water rights settlements:

> In the House, the Chairman of the Committee on the Budget may revise the allocations, aggregates, and other appropriate levels in this resolution for any bill, joint resolution, amendment, or conference report that would fulfill the purposes of the San Joaquin River Restoration Settlement Act or implement a Navajo Nation water rights settlement and other provisions authorized by the Northwestern New Mexico Rural Water Projects Act by the amounts provided in such measure if such measure would not increase the deficit or decrease the surplus for the period of fiscal years 2008 through 2013 or for the period of fiscal years 2008 through 2018.[21]

Reserve funds are not always required to be deficit-neutral. They may, instead, allow the levels of spending set forth in the budget resolution to be exceeded, as long as the policy legislation meets the conditions of the reserve fund. In some instances, the increases authorized by a reserve fund are limited to specified amounts.

End Notes

[1] U.S. Constitution, Article I, Section 9.
[2] U.S. Constitution, Article 1, Section 5.
[3] P.L. 93-344 as amended.
[4] For more information on the budget process generally, see CRS Report 98-721, *Introduction to the Federal Budget Process*, by Robert Keith.

[5] For more information on the appropriations process see CRS Report 97-684, *The Congressional Appropriations Process: An Introduction*, by Sandy Streeter.

[6] Under Section 301(a) of the Budget Act, four out-years is the minimum required, although the budget resolution may cover more than four. For example, the budget resolution for FY2002 (H.Con.Res. 83, 107th Congress) covered 10 out-years.

[7] These amounts are not enforced by points of order. For more information on functional categories see CRS Report 98-280, *Functional Categories of the Federal Budget*, by Bill Heniff Jr.

[8] These totals are named after Section 302(a) of the Budget Act (Titles I-IX of P.L. 93-344, 88 Stat. 297-332) as amended, which requires that the total budget authority and outlays set forth in the budget resolution be allocated to each House and Senate committee that has jurisdiction over specific spending legislation.

[9] U.S. Congress. Senate Committee on the Budget. *Committee Print to Accompany S.Con.Res. 70*. 110th Cong., 1st sess. S.Prt. 110-039 (Washington: GPO, 2008) p. 9.

[10] S.Con.Res. 13 (111th Congress), Sec. 606.

[11] S.Con.Res. 70 (110th Congress), Title IV.

[12] S.Con.Res. 70 (110th Congress), Sec. 402.

[13] For information on Presidential budget submission during years of transition, see CRS Report RS20752, *Submission of the President's Budget in Transition Years*, by Robert Keith.

[14] For example, see S.Con.Res. 13 (111th Congress), Sec. 401.

[15] These totals are named after Section 302(b) of the Budget Act which requires that the Appropriations Committees suballocate 302(a) allocations among their respective subcommittees.

[16] Such points of order may be waived by a special rule reported from the Rules Committee or by unanimous consent in the House. In the Senate, points of order may be waived by unanimous consent or by a 3/5 vote of Senators duly sworn and chosen (60 if no vacancies).

[17] In the House, Rule XXI, clause 2(f) provides that " ... it shall be in order to consider en bloc amendments proposing only to transfer appropriations among objects in the bill without increasing the levels of budget authority or outlays in the bill. When considered en bloc pursuant to this paragraph, such amendments may amend portions of the bill not yet read for amendment ... and shall not be subject to a demand for division of the question." For more information on offsets in the House, see CRS Report RL31055, *House Offset Amendments to Appropriations Bills: Procedural Considerations*, by Sandy Streeter.

[18] When Congress considers new revenue or direct spending legislation, CBO estimates the amount of revenues or outlays that would ensue if the measure were enacted. For revenues CBO uses estimates prepared by the Joint Committee on Taxation. These numbers are then measured against the baseline.

[19] For more information on the reconciliation process, see CRS Report 98-814, *Budget Reconciliation Legislation: Development and Consideration*, by Bill Heniff Jr..

[20] H.Con.Res. 95 (109th Congress), Sec. 201.

[21] S.Con.Res. 70 (110th Congress), Sec. 216.

CHAPTER SOURCES

The following chapters have been previously published:

Chapter 1 – This is an edited, excerpted and augmented edition of a United StatesCongressional Research Service publication, Report Order Code R40088, dated December 31, 2009.

Chapter 2 – This is an edited, excerpted and augmented edition of a United StatesCongressional Research Service publication, Report Order Code RL32747, dated January 4, 2010.

Chapter 3 – This is an edited, excerpted and augmented edition of a United StatesGovernment Accountability Office publication, Report Order Code GAO-10-468SP, dated January 2010.

Chapter 4 – This is an edited, excerpted and augmented edition of a Congressional Budget Office publication, dated May 2010.

Chapter 5 – This is an edited, excerpted and augmented edition of a United StatesCongressional Research Service publication, Report Order CodeR40472, dated June 9, 2009.

INDEX

D

E

F